Great Party Games

Great Party Games

Over 200 Games for Adults of All Ages

Gyles Brandreth

 **Robson Books**

This edition first published in Great Britain in 2000
by Robson Books, 10 Blenheim Court,
Brewery Road, London N7 9NT

A member of the Chrysalis Group plc

First published in hardback by Robson Books Ltd

ISBN 0 86051 672 5

Printed by
The Guernsey Press Co. Ltd,
Guernsey, Channel Islands.

Contents

Introduction

Since Adam and Eve first played Blind Man's Buff in the Garden of Eden, party games have been popular. And today they are more popular than ever before. Despite, or maybe in reaction to, the all-pervasive flood of mass entertainment available at the flick of a switch, when a number of people are gathered together the enlightened ones like nothing better than to play a parlour game. So no host or hostess, whether in the champagne and canapés or beer and beans categories, can afford to be without a good selection of games at his or her fingertips. And not only are games fun, they are good for us. As Molière said, 'Our minds need relaxation, and give way, unless we mix work with a little play.' And G.K. Chesterton quite properly described play as the true object of all human life. 'Heaven,' he said, 'is a playground.' Yes, party games are the nearest thing to nirvana that we've got.

The aim of the good games guide you now have in your hand is to provide a volume from which hosts and hostesses can choose the very game that will please their guests at any particular moment at any kind of party. For, in my view, whenever two or more are gathered together, it's party time – or ought to be.

I have tried to make this collection both catholic and comprehensible. It includes some of the old favourites Queen Victoria knew as a girl, plus many adult games quite unlike any that have been played before. I like to think it might find favour with both my elderly maiden aunt and my next-door neighbours, a young couple who work in the fashion industry, and whose parties are more likely to be graced by the music of Madonna than that of Mozart. There are games here for the innocent and the wicked, for the sober and the merry, for the prim and the permissive, for the athletic and the sedentary, for the extrovert and, yes, for the introvert too. The games are flexible: you can play them with assorted numbers and adapt the rules to suit your taste. Some have a competitive element, with prizes for the winners and forfeits for the losers, but they don't necessarily have to be played in this way. Whatever the mood or mix of the players, they should be able to find a game to suit them in the pages that follow. What's more, the games work. They have been tried out on many memorable evenings over the years by my family and friends, and naturally it is to these kind 'games guinea pigs' that this book is playfully dedicated.

G.B.

Guide to Symbols

The games have been divided into twelve sections to help hosts and hostesses select those best suited to the kind of party they are giving and the guests they are entertaining. The symbols are designed as a quick reference to the specific features of each particular game. This is what they mean.

∧	A game that is quite easy to pick up and quite easy to play.
∧ ∧	A game that is very easy to pick up and which any fool can play.
	A demanding game to pick up and play.
	A very demanding game to pick up and play.
	A game with risks (of all kinds), only to be played with the right people.
	A risky game (in many senses), only to be played with the right people.
	A game that is more fun when a few glasses of your favourite tipple have been consumed.
	One of the world's great games.

Ice-breakers

Soul Mates
Cinders' Slippers
Treasure Hunt
Who's Next?
Probing Partners
Odds On
Matchboxing
Pass the Fruit
Farmyard Frolic
Circle Talking
Apple Ducking
All Change
The Blanket Game

SOUL MATES △

Players: *any even number*
Equipment: *small pieces of paper or card*

This is a perfect getting-to-know-you game. As the guests arrive, the host or hostess gives each of them a small slip of paper or piece of card on which is written the name of a notorious lover. Each guest then has to set about finding his or her partner, not by shouting out: 'I'm Antony, where's Cleo?' but by going round the other guests and talking to them one by one. If obvious lovers are chosen, like Romeo and Juliet, or Catherine and Heathcliff, the company will have paired off before they are through their first cocktail. However, if care is taken in selecting the soul mates and Harold Nicolson has to discover Vita Sackville-West, Joe di Maggio, Marilyn Monroe, and Hiawatha, Minnehaha, the game will be a good deal more rewarding. If, by some chance, there are more women than men, one of the male guests can be Henry VIII, Bluebeard, or Warren Beatty. Should there be a plethora of men, one of the ladies could call herself Cynthia Payne, or even Beverly Nina Avery. Ms Avery, a barmaid from Los Angeles, has had fourteen husbands (five of which are alleged to have broken her nose) and is believed to be the world's most married woman.

CINDERS' SLIPPERS △ △

Players: *any even number*
Equipment: *none*

As the guests arrive, they are greeted by the host and hostess who are on their knees at the front door. They are on their knees in order to have quick and easy access to the feet of their friends. Every time a lady steps through the door, the host removes her left shoe. Every time a gentleman comes in, the hostess takes off his right shoe. As soon as everyone has arrived, the host and hostess put the whole collection of shoes in the middle of the room and invite everybody to pick up one shoe (not their own) and find a partner whose foot it will fit. The game is a perverse race, with the last person remaining with a foot unshod the winner. The prize is a sip of champagne from the shoe of the victor's choice (or, if preferred, red plonk from a glass). Considerate hosts will warn their guests so they can be sure to turn up in socks without holes and unladdered tights.

TREASURE HUNT △

Players: *any number*
Equipment: *small pieces of paper on which clues are written*

The opening moments of a party can be hell, for while the host is relieving guests of their coats and showing them where they can park their cars, and the hostess is in the kitchen cursing the soufflé that won't rise, the invited company are standing about, making faltering small talk and feeling lost. If the hosts can't be with their guests, they should at least leave them doing something. Why not leave them hunting for treasure? The hosts should scatter esoteric clues about the house, leading the guests, hunting individually or as a group, to further clues, and eventually to the treasure. The clues should not be made too complicated, or the guests will lose interest in both the game and the evening.

WHO'S NEXT 🖋

Players: *any number*
Equipment: *none*

Countless wheezes and ruses have been devised to help the forgetful remember the names of those to whom they have only just been introduced, but none is as effective as this farcical game. After the guests have all been introduced, they are seated in a circle. Just to make sure everyone has mastered everyone else's first name, each guest boldly declares his or her identity once more before the game begins. The host or hostess, who is seated in the circle with the guests, suddenly points a finger at one of them, mentioning his or her name and asking, 'Who's next?' Now comes the catch. If the host or hostess points with the right hand, the player pointed at must immediately point to some other player to his or her *right*, and call his or her name. If the host or hostess points with the left hand, the player pointed at must point to another player to his or her *left*, and call his or her name. The second player may point with either hand to the third player, but again, if he or she points with the left hand the third player calls out the name of a person to the left, and so on. Thus the host, Adam, might point at Eve with his right hand and say, 'Eve, who's next?' Eve would then point at Cain, who is to her right, with her left hand, and say, 'Cain'. Cain would then point at Abel, who is to his left, with his right hand and say, 'Abel'. And so it goes on. Any player who points in the wrong direction, forgets a name, falters, fumbles or falls to the ground, beating it with clenched fists, drops out.

PROBING PARTNERS ✍

Players: *any even number*
Equipment: *pencils and pieces of paper (optional)*

This is a good getting-to-know-you game for a largish party with a fair proportion of strangers. It won't work so well with family groups, or if most of the guests already know each other. The guests form two concentric circles, the women inside facing outwards and the men outside facing inwards. While the hostess sings 'Getting To Know You' from *The King and I*, or plays it, or another tune, on a tape or a piano, the circles move round in opposite directions. When the singing stops, everyone has two minutes in which to find out as much as possible about the person opposite. If anyone *is* facing someone already known, then the men all move round to the next person on their left. When the two minutes have passed, the singing or music starts and and the circles move on once more. When everyone appears to have met everyone else, the company, still in two concentric circles, is asked to sit on the floor. Everybody is then supplied with a pencil and piece of paper and given a further two minutes in which to write a brief but intimate biography of the individual who revealed most in the course of the game. The biographies are then read out and the most revelatory biographer, whose tale was obviously told to him by an idiot with a reckless disregard for the secrets of the boudoir, is the winner. Cautious hosts may prefer to keep out the competitive element and forgo the written biographies.

ODDS ON △

Players: *any number*
Equipment: *matchsticks or cocktail sticks*

In the initial stages of a party where nobody knows anybody, conversation can be awkward. 'And what do you do?' one guest asks another, only to hear an answer that leaves him none the wiser, such as, 'I'm a structural engineer.' This game is an excellent mixer, and gets the guests through that dangerous period of forced, faltering chit-chat. As the guests arrive, the host gives each of them ten matchsticks. The guest then takes a number of the matchsticks in one hand, closes the fingers over them, and holds out the clenched fist to another guest, demanding, 'Odd or even?' The other guest gives his or her answer, and if he or she has guessed correctly, the person holding the matchsticks gives one of them to him or her. This second guest then goes through the same routine with his or her own matchsticks. If the original questioner guesses incorrectly, he or she hands over another match, but if the guess was correct, then he or she collects a match from the opponent. Guests then circulate for five or ten minutes, demanding, 'Odd or even?' of anyone who takes their fancy. When the time is up, the player with the greatest number of matchsticks is the winner.

MATCHBOXING △ △

Players: *any even number*
Equipment: *two matchboxes*

Having emptied all the matches out, here is a use for the empty boxes, or at any rate their sliding covers. Players divide into two teams, each team standing in a straight line. The individual at the head of each team pushes the cover of a matchbox on to his or her nose and then turns to the person next in line and attempts to transfer the matchbox to the other person's nose *without using hands.* In this fashion the matchbox is passed from person to person down the line, and the first team to transfer it from one end of the team to the other, without dropping it or touching it with the hands, wins. If either of these two things happens, then the matchbox cover has to go back to the beginning and the team starts again. If possible, the host should pick teams with equally proportioned noses, so neither side gets all the advantageous Roman hooters, nor all the disastrous loose, flabby nostrils.

PASS THE FRUIT △ △ ✳

Players: *any number*
Equipment: *an orange or a banana*

This is a very intimate game, and can also be rather vulgar, depending on which version you play. At the end of it, people tend to feel they have known the other players for years, even though they have only met a few minutes ago. The players stand in a circle holding hands and pass an orange round from player to player, holding the fruit under their chins. Those caught using their hands, or who drop the orange, are disqualified. If you want to take the game further, you can then try passing the orange round the circle from knee to knee, though this is not easy for any women players wearing tight skirts. For the final stage of the game, the players should sit or lie on the floor, take off their shoes, and pass the fruit round holding it with their feet. If the players find passing an orange too difficult, they could try passing a banana.

FARMYARD FROLIC △

Players: *any number*
Equipment: *a number of small objects, such as sweets, coins or buttons*

This game is so silly it is guaranteed to unwind the wound-up, and soften up the starchy. Players divide into teams of three, four or five, one of whom is the leader, and the rest are animals of their own choosing. The host scatters around the house a large number of small objects, such as sweets or coins, and sets the team members, or 'animals', searching for the objects, leaving the team leaders sitting on a sofa. When a team member finds an object he or she makes a noise like the chosen animal until the team leader comes to collect it. After an agreed amount of time, say ten minutes, the team whose leader has the greatest number of objects, wins. An extra prize can be awarded to the team making the most original and lifelike animal noises. Most people can moo or bark, but how many can imitate a squirrel, a badger or a rutting stag?

CIRCLE TALKING 🎓

Players: *any even number*
Equipment: *a source of music*

For this admirable getting-to-know-you-and-getting-to-either-like-you-or-hate-you exercise, two concentric circles are formed, the men in the inner circle facing outwards and the women in the outer circle facing inwards. To the accompaniment of music the circles dance round in opposite directions. When the music stops everyone must talk to the person immediately opposite for two minutes on a topic to be announced by the host. The pairs must exchange views on the Prime Minister's walk, the latest episode of *Dallas*, the privatization of the electricity industry, on the advantages of vasectomy, or on 'my most embarrassing moment'. When the two minutes have passed, the music strikes up again and the circles dance round once more. Once all the topics, to say nothing of the players, have been exhausted, and everyone appears to have been exposed to the view of everyone else, the host announces the Moment of Truth. This 'moment' lasts for a minute, during the course of which the players rush about the room trying to catch hold of the individual with whom they feel most in sympathy. This is fine if A and B are mutually enchanted, but can be grim if A is pursuing B, while B is chasing C and C is crazy over A. A kind-hearted host, alarmed at the prospect of such Racinian triangles, can skip the Moment of Truth and simply regard the game as a sort of high-powered Paul Jones.

APPLE DUCKING △ △

Players: *any number*
Equipment: *one or more tubs of water and as many apples as there are guests*

The round, firm, fleshy fruit of a rosaceous tree may have been the cause of Adam's undoing, but an apple – or several apples – floating in a tub of water can be the making of an informal party. Place the tub or tubs on the floor – stand them on polythene sheets if you are worried about the carpet – and, as the guests arrive, get them to kneel down, bite into a bobbing apple and lift it clear. Nobody can have a drink without securing an apple – or losing his or her teeth in the attempt! An extravagant host might like to set the apples a-bobbing in a tub of red wine; the thoughtful host will provide bibs for the participants.

ALL CHANGE △ ☠

Players: *any even number*
Equipment: *two changing rooms*

Since people tend to hide behind their clothes (apart, that is, from Page Three girls), the host who wants to liberate his guests must persuade them to undress. But since most Anglo-Saxons are modest, and have to enjoy mostly cold and wet weather, Nude Parties and Underwear Parties are unlikely to be successful in Britain. Yet one of the best ways to unwind is to undress. And one of the best ways of getting to know someone is to put yourself in his or her shoes. This ice-breaking game combines the two. As the guests arrive, the men are sent off to one room and the women to another, in order to swap clothes with another guest. They then spend the evening in each other's outfits, freed from their own protective clothing and enchanted by the eccentricity of their own behaviour. It is an ideal game for the host who wants to give a 'swinging' party which no one will regret, because, while it appears devilishly daring, it is, in fact, absurdly innocent.

THE BLANKET GAME △ ☠

Players: *one or two, plus audience*
Equipment: *a blanket*

When Rupert Brooke referred to 'the rough male kiss of blankets' in his poem 'The Great Lover', he might well have had this effective warming-up frolic in mind. A player is selected and invited to sit in the middle of a room under a huge blanket. He or she is told that there is something he or she has, which must be passed to the assembled company before he or she is released. The poor player will start by passing out things like a wristwatch and jewellery, before starting to remove actual clothes. Then out will come one garment after another, until the player is sitting stark naked under the blanket, not having realized that the sought-after object was, in fact, the blanket itself. The game can only be played once in an evening and, even then, the victim must be chosen with care. An adventurous host may prefer to put *two* people underneath the blanket at the same time, of opposite or the same sex, depending on the kind of party it is.

Very Silly Games

Balloon Bashing
Goodies and Baddies
Squeak, Piggy, Squeak
The Picture Frame Game
Balloon Battle
Fanning the Kipper
Mummies
Nose Ball
Feather Race
Blindfold Drawing

BALLOON BASHING △

Players: *any number*
Equipment: *a blindfold, a balloon and a rolled-up newspaper*

The players stand in a circle. One player at a time is blindfolded and stands in the centre with a rolled-up newspaper. An inflated balloon is then placed somewhere in the circle, and the blindfolded player is told to 'Bash the balloon!' The player is allowed three goes at bashing the balloon with the rolled-up newspaper. He or she scores three points if it is bashed on the first attempt, two points if it is bashed on the second attempt, and one point if it is bashed on the third attempt. If the player fails to hit it, no points are scored. When all the players have had a go the player with the highest score is the winner. If there is a tie, the players can have a second go to find an eventual winner.

GOODIES AND BADDIES △ △

Players: *any even number*
Equipment: *a balloon*

Players are divided into two teams, the Goodies and the Baddies. The game should be played in a room without too many breakable ornaments! The Goodies are given the blown-up balloon, and it is their job to keep it airborne, while the Baddies have to try to burst it. However, the use of sharp or pointed instruments is forbidden, and the players are not allowed to molest one another. When the balloon has been burst, the teams can change roles and names and have a go with a second balloon.

SQUEAK, PIGGY, SQUEAK △ ♀

Players: *any number*
Equipment: *a blindfold and a cushion*

Surprisingly, this idiotic children's game is very popular with sophisticated adults. One player is blindfolded, and equipped with a cushion. He or she stands in the centre of a seated circle of the other guests. The blindfolded person is turned round two or three times so he is not sure of his whereabouts, and then has to grope his way towards one of the guests in the circle. Having found one, he places the cushion on that person's lap, sits on it, and calls out, 'Squeak, piggy, squeak!' The person being sat upon then has to squeak like a pig, and from the sound the blindfolded player has to guess whose lap he is sitting on. If he guesses correctly, the two players change places and the sat-upon- is blindfolded for the next round. If he does not, he goes off to seek another lap.

THE PICTURE FRAME GAME △ ♀

Players: *any number*
Equipment: *a large empty picture frame*

The players form a circle, in the centre of which, one by one, they take turns to hold up the picture frame so that it frames their face. They have to hold the picture frame – and a completely impassive and motionless face – for two minutes. If they flinch, move other than blinking, or giggle (and even inscrutable Orientals are usually reduced to helpless hysterics in under a minute) they give up the frame to the next person, and either lose a point or have to undertake a forfeit.

BALLOON BATTLE △ △

Players: *any number*
Equipment: *a blown-up balloon, a rolled-up newspaper and a piece of string for each player*

This exceedingly silly game is great fun to play. Each player ties a balloon with a piece of string to his or her ankle and, armed with a rolled-up newspaper, attempts to protect the balloon from other players' attempts to burst it, while at the same time trying to burst theirs. No balloons may be touched by hand or by pointed instruments. Any player whose balloon is burst is eliminated, and the last player left in is the winner.

FANNING THE KIPPER △

Players: *any number*
Equipment: *a 'kipper' cut out of newspaper, and a magazine or newspaper for each player, plus two long tapes or pieces of string*

The tapes or lengths of string are spread across opposite ends of the room, one being the starting line and one the finishing line. Players line up behind the starting line and place their 'kippers' with their tails just touching it. On the word 'Go!' each wafts the 'kipper' with the newspaper or magazine to propel it towards the finishing line, the one whose kipper crosses it first being the winner. Touching the kipper with the newspaper or magazine, with any part of the player's body, or with anything else, disqualifies a player, as does deliberately obstructing another player's progress.

MUMMIES △ ♀

Players: *any even number over four*
Equipment: *a roll of toilet paper for each couple*

This game has nothing to do with Mummies and Daddies, even if it is played in couples. In fact, it is the female of each couple who makes the male a mummy in this game. Players pair off into couples, and each female is given a roll of toilet paper. She then has three minutes in which to wrap her male partner from head to foot in toilet paper so that he resembles an Egyptian mummy. The couple judged to have produced the best mummy win.

NOSE BALL △

Players: *any number*
Equipment: *a ping-pong ball for each player, plus two long tapes or pieces of string*

As in Fanning the Kipper, the tapes or lengths of string are spread across opposite ends of the room as the starting and finishing lines. Each player has to put his or her ping-pong ball on the starting line, kneel down behind it, and on the word 'Go!' push the ball to the finishing line using only the nose. All those who touch the ball with anything other than their noses have to return to the starting line and begin all over again. The winner is the person whose ball crosses the finishing line first.

FEATHER RACE ☜♠♀

Players: *any number*
Equipment: *a plate and a feather for each player*

This is a lightweight game, suitable for feather brains and not-so-feather brains, all of whom, after a few glasses of wine, will find it hysterically funny. Each player is given a plate with a feather on it, and on the word 'Go!' all have to race to the finishing line as fast as their feathers will allow them. Feathers may not be touched by hand (or glued on to the plates!), and if one floats to the ground that player has to go back to the start line and begin all over again. It tends to be a question of more haste less speed. The winner is the first person to reach the finishing line with the feather still on the plate.

BLINDFOLD DRAWING

Players: *any number*
Equipment: *a blindfold, sheet of paper and a pencil for each player*

You don't have to be an artist in order to play this game – in fact, even if you are, your results are likely to be just as amusing as those of the less talented. All the players are each given a sheet of paper and a pencil, and securely blindfolded. Then they are told to draw a picture of the street they live in. They are told to draw their house, to add a tree or two to the garden, a car parked outside, two children playing with a dog, and so on. The host or hostess can be as devious and inventive as possible. When the drawings are finished, the blindfolds are removed, and everyone examines the results – which are usually hilarious!

Dramatic Games

Newspaper Fancy Dress
Charades
Adverbs Alive!
Crisis
Dumb Crambo
Fairy Tales
Doasyouwouldbedoneby
Acting Proverbs
Fancy Undress
Destination, Please
Emotional Mime
Mimic
Alibi
The Railway Carriage Game
Play Time
Proverbial Pantomime
Who Am I? Mark I
Who Am I? Mark II
Who Am I? Mark III

NEWSPAPER FANCY DRESS △

Players: *any number*
Equipment: *two newspapers and a supply of pins for each player*

Each player is given ten minutes to make a fancy-dress costume with two newspapers (preferably broadsheets) and a pile of pins, and, having created it, has to model it with appropriate gestures and actions in order that the rest of the guests can guess what it is meant to be. The player judged to have made the most ingenious costume, and shown it off to the best effect, wins.

CHARADES

Players: *any number*
Equipment: *none necessary, though dressing-up clothes can make it more fun*

There is no finer party game, none more entertaining, and none more popular, than Charades. The word derives from the Spanish *charrada*, which means the chatter of clowns, but in England in 1776 it came to mean a post-prandial indoor entertainment. Since then it has been one of our national pastimes, and no party is complete without it.

The guests are divided into teams. The first team retires to another room, to choose a word to dramatize, and to plan the performance to be given. The team's captain then returns to the room in which the other guests are assembled, and announces how many syllables there are in the word the team has chosen to dramatize, and in what order the syllables are to be dramatized. Various members of the team then come into the room and act, with or without dialogue, little scenes designed to give a clue to the sound of the syllables they are dramatizing. Each syllable is acted out individually then, finally, the word is performed as a whole. The rest of the guests watch the performance and try to guess each syllable as it is presented.

A variation on the traditional game involves the acting team deciding not on a mere word but on the title of a book, play or poem, or of a film, television programme or piece of music. They then work out how to act out the title, syllable by syllable or part by part, either using dialogue or – and it's funnier this way – by means of dumb show. Suppose the chosen title were *Romeo and Juliet* (Errol Flynn's favourite when he played the game, as he often did, in his Hollywood heyday), the players might stride about (roam), bray like donkeys (eeyore), hold hands (hand), admire their rings (jewel), and gobble an imaginary dish greedily (ate). Having decided how best to convey their title, the players perform their charade to the opposing team or teams. If the opponents guess the title before the charade is completed, they win. If they don't, they lose. In either case, it is another team's turn to leave the room and think of a title to act out.

With a small company, or with guests who don't like the idea of dividing up into teams, it is simpler, and just as much fun, to play Solo Charades, with individuals taking turns to act out the words or titles of their choice.

ADVERBS ALIVE! △

Players: *any number*
Equipment: *none*

While one player is out of the room, the remainder choose an adverb. When the outsider returns, he tells each player in turn to perform an action – it might be kissing the hostess, singing, mixing a cocktail, romping round the room on all fours – in the manner of the chosen word. The players undertake their task 'slowly', 'wearily', 'arrogantly', 'passionately', 'violently', 'prettily', as prescribed, and when each player has done his or her bit the outsider must guess the adverb. If he cannot, he must pay a forfeit.

The less obvious the adverb, the more entertaining the game. If the outsider asks one of the players to take off his wife's shoes and tickle her toes and the chosen adverb is something simple, such as 'sexily' or 'clumsily', the outsider is going to guess it

29

almost at once. However, if it is something more ingenious, such as 'sarcastically', 'inquisitively' or 'rumbustiously', the challenge is much greater.

CRISIS

Players: *any number*
Equipment: *none*

What would you do if the Duchess of York stopped you in the street and asked you what you thought of her clothes? What would you do if Joan Collins invited you to taste the intimacies of her boudoir? What would you do if you were stuck in a lift with Sylvester Stallone? These, and questions like them – what would you do if you went trouserless to work? – probably prey on the loftiest minds at some time or other. This game is designed to allay fears and suggest ways out of particular, peculiar predicaments.

One player is sent from the room, while the others choose a critical or embarrassing situation in which to place him or her. When the outsider returns, he or she goes to each of the other players in turn and asks them what they would do in certain circumstances, presenting different circumstances to each player. And the players, instead of giving pertinent answers, give answers that apply to the crisis they devised in the outsider's absence. From these answers, the outsider must guess what the agreed-upon crisis is. So, if the predicament you had agreed upon were that the outsider had accidentally poisoned the boss by putting rat poison in his tea instead of his medicine, and the outsider asked, 'What would you do if you found your wife in bed with the window cleaner?', you might reply, 'Ring for an ambulance,' or 'Get the next boat to Bolivia,' or 'Ask the Chairman for a rise.'

DUMB CRAMBO △

Players: *any even number*
Equipment: *none*

Three hundred years ago Samuel Pepys noted in his diary: 'From thence to the Hague, again playing at Crambo in the waggon.' Anything Pepys could do, you should be able to do better. And Dumb Crambo is undoubtedly a better game than Crambo. The players divide into two teams, one of which goes out of the room while the other chooses a word. When the outsiders return they are told a word which rhymes with the chosen one. They then guess the chosen word and mime an illustration of it. They are allowed three attempts. Anyone who speaks forfeits the game for his or her team. Crambo can be played without the dumb show, as it was until the eighteenth century, with the outsiders simply guessing at the chosen word after hearing another word that rhymes with it, but it is the mime which gives the game its bite.

FAIRY TALES 🎓

Players: *any number*
Equipment: *none*

Players divide into two teams and re-enact famous fairy tales, devising their dialogue as they go along. But they must assume their dramatic roles not as themselves, but as well-known personalities of the day. So, were *Little Red Riding Hood* the chosen fairy tale, the part of Red Riding Hood might be played by the Princess of Wales, the Wolf by Norman Tebbit, and the Woodcutter by Robert Maxwell. Once the first team has performed its tale, the opponents must guess which fairy story it was and the double identity of all the players. The game can be given an added twist by requiring the players to act their story in the manner of a particular film director. Dick Whittington, *à la* Ken Russell or Federico Fellini, with Terry Wogan as Dick and Dame Edna Everage as his Puss, offers intriguing dramatic possibilities.

DOASYOUWOULDBEDONEBY △

Players: *any number*
Equipment: *cards bearing each guest's name, plus pencils for each*

Charles Kingsley described Mrs Doasyouwouldbedoneby, the water babies' friend, as 'the loveliest fairy in the world'. The host and hostess who regularly play this game on their guests deserve no such accolade. It is a mean game, not enjoyed by many, yet still very popular in certain circles. Before the guests arrive, cards must be prepared, each bearing the name of a guest. The cards are separated according to sex, with those bearing the names of male guests being put in one box, and those bearing the names of female guests being put in another. When it is time to play the game, each woman is invited to draw a man's card, and each man to draw a woman's. Now instruct everyone to write on the card some action, stunt, exhibition or other form of indoor entertainment he or she would like to see performed. Everyone will assume that the person named on the card will be expected to do the dirty work. But – surprise, surprise, instead of collecting the cards and passing them to the people whose names they bear, the host will ask each player in turn to read out what they have written and will then say, 'If that's what you want, let's see *you* do it!' So the hapless Eve, who wanted Adam to rub noses with the hostess, has to do so herself. And the luckless Antony, who visualized Cleopatra doing the splits while singing the chorus of ''Twas on the Good Ship Venus', must undertake the desperate deeds himself. Of course, the nice guests who really do do as they would be done by, come off lightly. It is only to the horrid ones, and to those trying to be extra clever, that the exigencies of Fate bring their revenge.

ACTING PROVERBS 🎓

Players: *any number*
Equipment: *none*

The players are divided into teams of three or four people. One team is sent out of the room to think of a well-known proverb to act out for the others to guess. That team then returns to the room, and acts out the proverb in one scene. The team that guesses the proverb takes a turn to act out a proverb of its choice. If no one guesses the proverb, the team that acted it has a second go.

Anyone stuck for proverbs might consider the following:

A stitch in time saves nine.
Too many cooks spoil the broth.
A rolling stone gathers no moss.
Many hands make light work.
Don't count your chickens before they're hatched.
Look before you leap.

FANCY UNDRESS 🎓

Players: *any number*
Equipment: *none*

This is not the risqué game its name implies, for the undressing is purely metaphorical. Guests are invited to attend decked out not in the clothes, but in the *personalities* of famous figures of fact or fiction. Adam comes dressed as himself, but behaves in the manner of the Marquis de Sade. Eve comes as she is, but behaves like Alexis Carrington. At the end of the party, everybody must guess who everyone else was pretending to be. If the strain of impersonation becomes too much – and an evening as Prince Andrew or Margaret Thatcher would tax anyone's inner resources – the moment of psychological unmasking can be brought forward by an hour or so.

DESTINATION, PLEASE △

Players: *any number*
Equipment: *none*

This is a team game that combines the skills of mime and spelling. One team goes out of the room and chooses the name of a town or city to which its members are travelling. On their return, they mime one action for each letter in the name of their destination, and that action must begin with the letter they are miming. They can either mime as a team or let each member mime a different letter, though the latter is more fun. If the destination chosen were Florence, for example, they might mime fighting, lying, opening something, rowing, exploring, nesting, crying, and echoing. When all the mimes are completed, the audience must guess the destination, with a time limit imposed if necessary. They may ask for a particular mime to be repeated, and the actor must repeat it in exactly the same manner as he or she first performed it. If they guess the destination correctly, then they choose their own destination to mime. If not, the first team has a second turn.

EMOTIONAL MIME ▱ ☠

Players: *any number*
Equipment: *none*

One player mimes an emotion – anything from love or lust to fear or fury – to the assembled company, who must guess what emotion he or she is miming. The player must mime alone, without benefit of props and without involving any other individual in the mime.

The game can be given an added edge if the player is required to mime the emotion which he or she feels dominates any one of the other individuals in the room. In this instance the company has to guess not only the emotion but also the identity of the individual in whom it is supposed to be dominant. If the company includes too many neurotics, this variation is not to be encouraged!

MIMIC △

Players: *any number*
Equipment: *prepared cards*

Before the guests arrive, the host prepares a card for each. On it, he writes a brief description of a character, or the name of a well-known public figure. If he suspects that his guests will not make marvellous mimics, he is best advised to put down simple descriptions, such as 'gay glazier', 'lager lout' or 'fading film star', but if he feels his guests are a talented crowd he can be more specific, listing Barbara Bush, Mikhail Gorbachev, Edwina Currie, Richard Branson, Anneka Rice, and the like. When the time comes to play the game each guest is given a nursery rhyme to recite – 'Little Jack Horner' is a good one – and told to draw one of the prepared cards. The guest then has to read the verse in the manner of the character named on the card, and the audience must guess who he or she is mimicking. Nobody wins, but a good time is had by all.

ALIBI 🎓

Players: *five or more*
Equipment: *none*

Care must be taken when choosing to play this game. Any lawyers among the guests may be so good at it they spoil it for the others, and anyone, such as the newly divorced, who has been involved in recent litigation, may find it depressing. But it is a fascinating game to play.

Adam and Eve are sent from the room and given ten minutes in which to concoct a watertight alibi. They must pretend they were together for twenty-four hours, and must agree between themselves as to exactly what happened throughout that time. When they have settled their alibi, Adam is brought back into the room where he is questioned closely by the assembled company for five minutes. Eve is then brought in and questioned. The aim of the game is to break the alibi by making Eve say something that doesn't tally with what Adam said. If she fails to corroborate Adam's story, both must undertake a forfeit.

THE RAILWAY CARRIAGE GAME △ ⚘

Players: *four or more*
Equipment: *none*

Two players are chosen, and each is given a secret phrase or sentence. Adam's might be, 'There is no alternative,' and Eve's, 'You're never alone with a loofah.' Armed with these phrases, Adam and Eve climb into an imaginary railway carriage and converse for five minutes. During that time they each must slip their phrase into the conversation as discreetly as possible. At the end of the journey, which is watched by the rest of the giggling company, Adam must guess what Eve's phrase was, and Eve must guess Adam's. This is one of the world's great games, which was played at British spy schools during the First and Second World Wars.

PLAY TIME △

Players: *any number over eight*
Equipment: *two or three identical bundles of assorted items*

The bundles, which might contain odd things like a doll, a sock, a boiled egg, a pencil, a menu, an ear-ring and a copy of *The Sun*, have to be prepared in advance. Guests are divided into two or three teams, and each team is given a bundle, without its contents being divulged. The teams are sent into separate rooms and each is told to prepare a short play, involving every member of the team and all the props in the bundle. They have ten minutes in which to script and rehearse their productions (they might find pencils and paper handy for the former) and then have to present their dramas in turn before the other teams.

PROVERBIAL PANTOMIME 🎓

Players: *any even number*
Equipment: *pieces of paper and pencils for each player*

Players are divided into two teams, and each player in each team writes down on a piece of paper a reasonably well-known proverb or maxim. The teams then exchange proverbs and the first player in the first team has to act out, in pantomime, the proverb he or she has been given. From this performance the player's team mates have to guess the proverb, and if they do so, the team gains a point. Though the teams are only allowed one guess and one minute for their deliberations, and may not put any questions to the player performing the mime, they are allowed to ask him or her to repeat the mime *once* if they are unable to agree on the proverb without an encore. If then they still cannot agree, the members of the opposing team, *excepting* the player who chose the proverb in question, can have a go at guessing. The players take it in turn to act out their proverbs, and the team that gains the greatest number of points wins. As their prize, the victors are allowed thirty seconds in which to blow proverbial raspberries at the vanquished. This is the best part of the game.

WHO AM I? MARK I △

Players: *three or more*
Equipment: *none*

One member of the party is told to leave the room, and not listen at the keyhole, while the remainder decide what famous person he or she is to be on his or her return. Once they have decided, the player can return, and by asking the rest of the guests questions requiring Yes or No answers must do his or her best to establish the identity. The player can ask each member of the party three questions, after which he or she must do an impersonation of whoever he or she thinks it is. There is a story that when Germaine Greer played this game, the players chose the identity of Germaine Greer for her. When she returned to the party, put her questions and heard the party's answers, she proceeded to impersonate Joan of Arc.

WHO AM I? MARK II 🖎

Players: *three or more*
Equipment: *none*

The game is given an engaging twist if the assembled company does not think of a famous person at all, but agrees to answer the player's questions in a special way. For example, when the player puts a question ending in a consonant ('Am I religious?') the answer is No; when the question ends with a vowel ('Am I a national hero?') the answer is Yes; when it ends with a 'y' ('Am I sexy?') the answer is Yes and No.

Despite the fact that no one is in the company's mind at all, the player will still attempt to impersonate somebody at the end of the question time.

WHO AM I? MARK III 🖎

Players: *four or more*
Equipment: *none*

The game can be further complicated and enlivened if the assembled company, while not actually thinking of a famous person, answers the player's questions in another, yet more ingenious, way. The members of the company must answer the player's questions as if the non-existent 'famous person' were the individual who is actually sitting immediately on their left. To the question, 'Am I a member of the Royal Family?' the answer is easy to give. Either your neighbour is Princess Michael of Kent or she's Aggie Brown. If the former, the answer is Yes. If the latter, No. But if the lady on your left is your mistress, not your wife, and the question is, 'Am I a notorious nymphomaniac?' a straightforward answer may be more difficult to come by. However, honesty is essential if the game is to succeed at all.

As before, when the player has asked everyone three questions, he or she must impersonate the famous figure believed to be the answer.

Truth Games

The Truth Game
All Lies
J'Accuse!
Analysis
The Common Man Game
Extremity
Ideal Identities
Liberation!
Murder Plot
Personality Swap
Regression
Statements
The Freud Game
Trauma

THE TRUTH GAME 🤫 ☠️ ☠️ 🍷

Players: *any number*
Equipment: *none*

This game is exactly what its title implies. The players must promise to speak the truth, the whole truth and nothing but the truth, in answer to any question of any kind. That's all there is to it. It is a game for devoted soul-barers and much easier to play with people you don't know well than with your loved ones. Those with a tendency, on the morning after, to regret the night before, should give it a miss.

ALL LIES △

Players: *any number*
Equipment: *none*

Surprisingly, this game is harder to play than the Truth Game, for it requires the players *never* to speak the truth, which is harder than it sounds. For the length of the evening, or for merely an hour, if the going gets too tough, the truth is impermissible. In the course of the conversation, if any guest suspects another guest of having told the truth, he is duty bound to report the truthful guest to the host, who will oblige the guilty party to undertake a forfeit – most probably an impersonation of George Washington.

J'ACCUSE! △

Players: *any number*
Equipment: *a stool; pencil and paper*

The players sit in a circle, in the middle of which is placed the stool, which is called the Stool of Repentance. One of the party volunteers to leave the room, while another goes round to those seated and collects 'evidence' against the culprit. If there is a large gathering it is as well to note it down on a piece of paper, writing the accuser's name beside each accusation. The outsider is then brought back in and seated on the stool. The person who collected the accusations addresses him or her: 'Prisoner on the Stool of Repentance, those gathered around you accuse you of being a gossip, of not paying your Income Tax, of telling malicious lies about your boss, of committing adultery with the dustman' - and so on. The prisoner must try to guess who made which charges, and as soon as he or she matches an accusation with an accuser, he or she is released. The revealed accuser becomes the new prisoner and has to leave the room while fresh evidence is gathered against him or her.

ANALYSIS

Players: *any number*
Equipment: *a chaise longue (or a sofa)*

Psychoanalysis tends to be fashionable at some periods and not at others, but taken light-heartedly it is certainly fun. Everyone can enjoy this version of it, even if it doesn't cure their psychological problems. A 'patient' is chosen and invited to lie down on the chaise longue, while the others play at being analysts and fire intimate questions at their victim, who is required to answer truthfully. After ten minutes of questioning, the analysts each outline their diagnoses of the patient's problems, and the one whom the patient feels is nearest the psychological mark is the winner.

A less potentially traumatic variation of the game involves each player writing down a brief description of his or her most memorable dream, and then getting fellow players to interpret it.

THE COMMON MAN GAME 🎭🦢

Players: *any number*
Equipment: *none*

Role-playing is said to be remarkably liberating, and this is a simple role-playing game with a difference. The guests are invited to the party, not as themselves, nor as Napoleon or Bismarck, nor even as Roland Rat or Dame Edna Everage, but as Mr or Mrs or Miss or Ms Nobody. The game's only rule is that the players may not be themselves, nor anyone they know. They must be ordinary individuals and must live their chosen characters to the life, supplying a name, family, career and complete historical and psychological background for themselves. If you hate yourself and long to lose yourself in someone else's identity, this is the game for you.

EXTREMITY 🍸 ☠ ☠ 🍷

Players: *any number*
Equipment: *none*

Players are divided into two teams, who take it in turns to behave in the manner dictated by their very *best* and their very *basest* instincts. For half an hour, the members of one team will give way to their meanest and lowest whims, while their opponents will be as high-minded and virtuous as their natures allow. When the time is up, the roles are reversed. So Adam could spend thirty minutes indulging in gluttony and stuffing his face with food, followed by thirty minutes in the guise of everybody's personal friend, listening sympathetically to their tales of personal tragedy. And Eve could give herself over to half an hour of unremitting bitchiness, followed by half an hour of singing 'Abide With Me' in the hope of salvaging a few lost souls.

Nobody wins this game, but it is an excellent way of getting up-tight individuals to doff the straitjacket of conventional behaviour.

IDEAL IDENTITIES ◌ ✄

Players: *any number*
Equipment: *none*

This is a consoling game, a marvellous therapy for anyone going through an identity crisis. The players sit in a circle and think of the character, in fact or fiction, they would most like to be. Having chosen their ideal identities, each player is questioned in turn by the other players who have to guess the name of the character in question. When it has been discovered that a certain player would love to be or have been Bertrand Russell or Elizabeth Bennett or Walter Gabriel or Elton John or Mae West or Noah, then that player has to give the reason why. This is a magnificent game if the players are honest, but feeble if they try to think of 'clever' or 'funny' characters and insist on wanting to be Noddy or Vlad the Impaler. It is a consoling game, because, however much you hate your identity, when you stop to think about it, it is almost impossible to think of anyone else's that you might really prefer.

LIBERATION! ✄☠🍷

Players: *any number*
Equipment: *pencils and pieces of paper for each guest*

The host or hostess puts two questions to the guests: 'What in the world would you most like to do?' and 'What would you most like to do here and now?' The guests are given a moment to consider the questions, and then invited to write down the answers on the pieces of paper provided. The papers are then collected, shuffled and redistributed. Each player then takes it in turn to read out the answer to the first question, and then actually undertakes whatever is prescribed in answer to the second question. Of course, feeble-spirited hosts, lacking the courage of their convictions, wouldn't force their guests to perform *all* the deeds described in the second set of answers, because some players might not feel up to whisking the hostess off to bed, getting blind drunk, or smashing all those ghastly mantelpiece ornaments. The host also has to hope that his guests are enjoying the party, because it would be embarrassing if someone wrote 'go home'. When all the answers have been read out or performed, players must guess exactly who wanted to do what.

MURDER PLOT 🖂🎝

Players: *any number*
Equipment: *none*

A game for the eerie early hours, this macabre exercise has a gruesome fascination. The players, sitting in a totally darkened room, take it in turns to describe the way in which they would choose to commit the perfect murder – and the victim of their crime has to be someone in the room. To hear a woman planning the murder of her husband is riveting, especially for the husband. This is one of the few spoken games in which it is an advantage to have a stammer. Curiously, the less articulate the murderer, the more telling his narrative. Girls have been known to faint as their boyfriends stuttered over the cyanide.

PERSONALITY SWAP 🖂🎝 ☠

Players: *any number*
Equipment: *none*

If played with honesty this can be a grimly revealing game. For the length, say, of the soup course, the guests must swap personalities with their partners and behave in exactly the way they believe their partners would behave. So Adam becomes Eve, and vice versa. Naturally, the better the partners know each other the more devastating the result. And when played by a couple having dinner *à deux*, the effect can be devastating.

REGRESSION △ ♀

Players: *any number*
Equipment: *jelly, jam and rosehip syrup, if taking it seriously!*

This is a game for people who had happy childhoods – or who *think* they had happy childhoods – and rue the day when society made them put away childish things. For the duration of the game (and players need at least half an hour to get warmed up) everyone returns to the age of their choice. Back to puberty! Back to the nursery! Even back to the womb! The players must simply behave as they remember behaving – or as they think they remember behaving – as they did when children, toddlers or babies. It is entertaining even if played alone!

The thoughtful hostess will contact the guests beforehand and do her best to provide appropriate fare, as outlined above, though this is not absolutely necessary.

STATEMENTS △ △ *or* 🐿 🐿

Players: *any number*
Equipment: *pencil and paper for each player*

This game is very popular in the Georgetown district of Washington DC; in Cambridge, Massachusetts; in North Oxford; and in certain parts of London, notably Barnes, Camden, Kentish Town and, when they're trying, Highbury and Muswell Hill. Of course, in these high-minded quarters the players don't realize that they're playing a game. In other, less intellectually pretentious parts of the world, the game has to be *organized*. The host or hostess invites the guests to write down on their piece of paper the most important statement in the world. It can be about anything, provided the author believes it is of truly cosmic significance and contains a basic truth. The statements are then collected, shuffled and read out, points being awarded for 'significance' and 'truth'. Dictionaries of quotations and pocket editions of Kant and Wittgenstein are not allowed.

THE FREUD GAME 🎓 🎓 ☠ 🍷

Players: *any number*
Equipment: *pencil and paper for each player*

As Ken Dodd is fond of remarking: 'The trouble with Freud is that he never played the Glasgow Empire Saturday night.' He is referring to Sigmund, not Clement, of course. Had Freud so performed, he might have persuaded his audience to play this game, in which nobody wins, but much is revealed. Quite simply, the host, donning smoking jacket, grizzled beard and guttural mid-European accent – not essential, but they help with the atmosphere – tells a story and invites the guests to fill in the gaps on paper as they feel most appropriate. At the end of the game the bits the guests have written down are read out and publicly interpreted.

At their simplest, the story and interpretations might go like this: You are walking through a wood, what are the trees like? (If you write them down as having thick trunks and being leafy, you are trusting; if you see them as thin and bare you are not.) You look up at the sky, what is it like? (If it's clear and blue, you're optimistic; if stormy and grey, you may be a manic depressive.) On the ground, by one of the trees, you discover a key. What is it like? (A simple Yale key indicates an unquesting, unimaginative personality; an ornate, elaborate key reveals an ambitious, inquiring mind.) You see an animal in the clearing, what is it? (If it's a mouse, you're timid; if it's a tiger, you're not.) You come across a pool, what do you do? (The water is indicative of your attitude to sex, so if you dive straight in and splash about enthusiastically, you should be OK; if you teeter timidly around the edge, you're in trouble; and if, Christ-like, you walk straight across it, God help you!) Eventually you come out of the wood and find yourself stepping into a totally new territory, what is it like? (Whatever you describe reveals your attitude to death.)

Both the story and the interpretations can be greatly extended and amplified, depending on how well you know your Freud. And your guests.

TRAUMA

Players: *any number*
Equipment: *none*

The players form two teams and depart into separate rooms. The first team decides on a traumatic experience for a particular member of the second team. The players return and the leader of the first team whispers the nature of the experience to the traumatized member of the second team, who then has to answer questions from his or her team-mates who have to guess the cause of the trauma. The traumatized individual may only answer the questions with a Yes or No, and his colleagues may only put twenty questions to him. Only truly traumatic experiences, likely to disturb the mind and nerves of a person and induce hearty hysteria, are allowed. To discover that your father was your brother and your sister was your mother could be counted as truly traumatic, whereas getting the hiccups at a funeral couldn't – unless it happened to be *your* funeral.

Romping Games

Are You There, Moriarty?
Blind Man's Buff
Hunt the Thimble
Kangaroo Racing
Bonnet Race
Deadpan
The Horror Game
Murder in the Dark
Execution
Front and Back Race
Ankle Race
Winking
Find the Leader
Light and Shade
Over the Sticks
Up Jenkins
Pan-tapping
Royal Court
Sardines
Witch Hunt

ARE YOU THERE, MORIARTY? △

Players: *two, plus audience*
Equipment: *two rolled-up newspapers and two blindfolds*

None but the very lame can fail to enjoy a good romp and, with a game like this one, adults of all ages can recapture the kind of innocent pleasure they thought they had lost at puberty. Inside every grim-faced grown-up there is a raving romper dying to get out, and the advantage of this game is that the reluctant romper isn't thrown in at the deep-end. He or she can stand back and watch others play and join in when the mood is right.

Two players are blindfolded and induced to lie flat on the floor, face-down, each grasping the other's left wrist with his or her left hand, and holding a rolled-up Sunday newspaper in the right hand. One says, 'Are you there, Moriarty?' and the other replies 'Yes' in one place and then rolls quickly to another. The inquirer lets fly with the rolled newspaper and attempts to hit the enemy on the head with one blow. Players take it in turns to ask the crucial question and sock the enemy. The first to fetch the other a clean swipe on the head is the victor.

The game – as its name implies – was devised in the late nineteenth century, at the time when the British public (or at least that part of it which read the *Strand Magazine*) was deeply shocked by the reported murder of Sherlock Holmes by the notorious Professor James Moriarty, 'the Napoleon of Crime'. Of course, Holmes and Moriarty didn't set about each other with rolled-up Sunday newspapers on that eventful day at the Reichenbach Falls, nor was Holmes really murdered, but it is nonetheless fitting that the encounter between the two giants should be commemorated by such an entertaining game. It is only a trifle, yet, as Holmes remarked on an earlier occasion, 'It has long been an axiom of mine that the little things are infinitely the most important.'

BLIND MAN'S BUFF △ △

Players: *any number*
Equipment: *one blindfold*

This is probably the oldest party game of all. It is almost certainly connected with the early rites of human sacrifice, and undoubtedly dates back to the time of the blind god Odin, the chief deity of Norse mythology. Through the centuries it has been known as 'Billie Blind', 'Blind Polmie', 'Hoodle Cum Blind' and 'Blind Harrie'. It is an entertaining romp, for all its bloody and godly past. A blindfolded player, posing as Odin, rushes about the room trying to catch hold of one of the other, sighted, players, who scramble, crawl and dodge out of his way. When the blindfolded man catches a sacrificial victim, he has to guess who it is, and if he's right the two change places.

HUNT THE THIMBLE △

Players: *three or more*
Equipment: *a thimble, or other small object*

This, too, is a classic party game. All the players except one go out of the room, while the one remaining 'hides' the thimble, or other small object, such as a pencil sharpener. It should not really be hidden but should be placed in some inconspicuous spot where, though not immediately noticeable, it will be visible to all players. The other players are then called back into the room and begin to hunt the thimble. As soon as a player spots it, he or she sits down, without saying anything or drawing attention to its location. The last player to spot the thimble and sit down is the loser, and he or she hides the thimble for the next round. The game does not have a winner.

KANGAROO RACING △ ∧

Players: *any number*
Equipment: *one inflated balloon per player*

This game could just as well appear in the 'Very Silly Games' category, as, in common with most games involving balloons, it *is* very silly. Players line up at the start, each with a balloon between the knees, and on the word 'Go!' must start hopping down the course like kangaroos, being careful not to drop the balloons as they go. Any player who drops a balloon must catch it, put it back between their knees, and start racing again from the point where the balloon fell. The first player to reach the finish with the balloon intact wins. Those who burst their balloons are disqualified.

BONNET RACE △ △

Players: *any even number*
Equipment: *two outrageous bonnets, and two huge pairs of bedsocks*

The players divide into two teams and line up in rows. The leader of each team dons an outrageous bonnet – Ascot at its most ridiculous – and ties the bonnet's ribbons (for it must have ribbons) underneath his or her chin. Number two in each team undoes the ribbons, puts on the bonnet, ties the ribbons, and so on down the line. The first team to cover every head wins. An entertaining variation, for experienced rompers, not suffering from slipped discs and varicose veins, is to give each team an enormous pair of bedsocks as well. In this case, the leader must put on and tie the bonnet *and* put on the bedsocks, which number two takes off and puts on his or her own feet, and so on. In this case, players have to remove their own shoes first, of course.

DEADPAN △ △

Players: *any number*
Equipment: *none*

A game for stoics who must sit on the floor cross-legged and in a tightly knit circle. A leader is chosen who nudges the player on his left, who nudges the player on *his* left, and so on round the circle. When the nudge reaches the leader, he tweaks the ear of the player on his left, who tweaks the ear of the player on *his* left, and again, so on round the circle. Next time the leader pulls his neighbour's nose, or blows in his ear, or kisses his brow, or tickles him under the armpit or whispers something rude or witty to him. Whatever the leader does, the others must do in quick succession. Speed is essential. Anyone who even smiles, let alone snickers, giggles, has hysterics or a minor attack of St Vitus's dance, is disqualified and leaves the circle. Whoever laughs last, wins, and is greeted by the others as a latter-day Zeno and a humourless bore.

THE HORROR GAME △ 💀

Players: *any number*
Equipment: *various – see below*

Not so much a jolly game, this, more a ghastly experience. The guests gather round a table in complete darkness, and the host, putting on a 'Man in Black' voice, tells them the story of the murder that was committed in that very room on the spot where they are now sitting. He describes the murder in a way which would have warmed the heart of Dr Crippen, had he had one, and which should chill his audience to the very core. He goes on to tell how the murderer, having killed his victim, dismembered the body in order to hide it. As each grisly part of the corpse is mentioned, the host passes it round the assembled guests for inspection. This is where the equipment comes in. It must all have been carefully prepared in advance. The victim's head can be a carefully carved turnip, with wool 'hair' added for verisimilitude; his hand, a clammy rubber glove stuffed with sand and tied at the wrist; his ears, dried figs or apricots; his eyes, peeled grapes; his brains, a wet sponge; his tongue, a slice of cold meat – and so on. It is a very nasty game!

When the ghastly tale is concluded, the lights are switched on. The host may find his guests in a hurry to leave; indeed, playing it is a good way of losing your friends. If you have an immensely wealthy and aged relative who stubbornly refuses to meet his or her Maker, it might be a good game for them, too.

MURDER IN THE DARK 📜 ❀

Players: *six or more*
Equipment: *a slip of paper for each player and a hat to draw them out of*

This is another chilling game, not for those with weak hearts. As many slips of paper as there are players are dropped in the hat. All but two of the slips are blank, but one bears a cross, which means that the player who draws it is the Murderer; and one bears a circle, and the player who draws that is the Detective. He or she announces the fact to the company, but the Murderer keeps silent. All the lights in the house are then turned off, and the players spread themselves around the house. The Murderer, black heart beating faster and faster, creeps through the gloom until a likely victim is found. The murderer seizes the hapless player by some part of his or her body, and whispers, 'You're dead!' whereupon the victim lies down, and screams and screams and *screams*. The Murderer rushes stealthily away. On hearing the screams, the Detective switches on the lights and rushes to the spot they are coming from. Everyone except the Murderer must remain still from the moment the screams sound.

After viewing the body, the Detective notes the positions of the various suspects, then gathers them round the corpse for questioning. Each player must answer truthfully, except the Murderer, who can lie as much as he or she likes, until asked directly, 'Are you the Murderer?' when the answer must be 'Yes.' If there are fewer than ten players, the Detective is only allowed two guesses at the Murderer's identity. If there are more than ten players, he or she can have three guesses. If the Detective fails to spot the inconsistencies in the Murderer's story, or if he or she fails to detect the Murderer's guilty smirk, the criminal proudly announces himself, and the Detective promptly goes off to seek a transfer from CID to Traffic Control.

EXECUTION △ △

Players: *four to six*
Equipment: *string; a black hood if available*

This game is less sinister than it sounds, for it is only the tips of the fingers that are in danger. The players sit in a circle, with the tips of their raised forefingers meeting in the centre. The executioner stands outside the circle, and should be wearing a black hood if he takes the game seriously. He slips a running noose made with string around the assembled fingertips and holds up the end of the string. At a certain moment he cries, 'Death!' and jerks up the string. The players whip their fingers away, but anyone whose reflexes are slow and whose finger gets caught in the noose is considered 'executed' - and can be sent off to make the coffee.

FRONT AND BACK RACE △

Players: *any even number*
Equipment: *two soup tureens, chamber pots or other containers, plus a number of assorted objects (see below)*

Two teams of even numbers stand sideways in line. On the floor by the leader of each team are two soup tureens, or other large containers, one empty, the other containing a dozen or more objects of various shapes and sizes, from a drawing pin and a lemon squeezer to a pipe and a hard-boiled egg. There should be at least three times the number of objects that there are members of the team, and the trickier the objects are to handle the more entertaining will be the game. A wet bar of soap, an open bottle of ink, a peeled banana and a hot potato are ideal. On the starting signal, the leader picks up one object at a time and passes it to the second person in the team, who passes it to the third, and so on down the line. When the object reaches the last player he or she begins to pass it back up the line *behind his or her back*, so that at the same time as objects are being passed along the line in front of the players, objects are travelling in the reverse direction behind them. Most players, having only two hands, find the exercise trickier than it sounds. It is quite as difficult as trying to pat the head while rubbing the stomach. When the leader receives the objects behind his back he puts them into the second, empty, tureen. The first team which transfers all its objects from one tureen to the other wins.

ANKLE RACE △

Players: *two or more*
Equipment: *none*

This is strictly for the agile and energetic. The players line up at the starting line and get into racing position, bending forward with a hand on each ankle. On the word 'Go!' they set off down the course racing as fast as they can, keeping hold of their ankles all the time. Any player who lets go of an ankle, even for a moment, or who trips and falls, must return to the starting point and begin all over again. The first player to cross the finishing line is the winner.

WINKING △

Players: *ten or more*
Equipment: *half as many chairs as players, plus an extra chair*

This game is quite good as an ice-breaker, as well as being a jolly romping game to help the evening go with a swing. The chairs are made into a circle facing inwards, and the girls and women sit on every chair except one. The boys and men stand behind the chairs, including the empty one, with their hands resting on the backs of the chairs but not touching the girls.

The man or boy standing behind the empty chair starts the game by winking at one of the girls. She must immediately try to dash from her chair to the empty one, but the boy standing behind her must try to stop her before she takes off by putting his hands on her shoulders. If he succeeds, the girl must remain seated, and the boy behind the vacant chair has to try winking at another girl. If, however, the girl does get away, the boy who failed to stop her has to try winking at one of the other girls. A few goes will soon show that it is the quick, subtle wink that wins the girl!

Once the girls have been winked at, they should change places with the boys, who should sit down and let the girls wink at them.

FIND THE LEADER △

Players: *six or more*
Equipment: *none*

This game, which is fairly silly, is also quite a challenging test of observation. One player is sent out of the room, and the other players select a leader. The leader performs some repetitive action, such as rubbing the nose, scratching the head, tapping the foot, or whatever, which the other players all copy. The outsider is summoned back into the room, where he or she finds all the other players busily rubbing or scratching or tapping. Suddenly the leader switches to some different action and the other players immediately follow his or her lead. The leader initiates different actions at frequent intervals. The outsider, by observing closely all the players, has to determine which of them is the leader. Each player has a turn at being the outsider.

LIGHT AND SHADE △

Players: *any number*
Equipment: *a white sheet and a lamp or torch*

In the days when people had roaring fires in their drawing-rooms, this was a very popular game. Now that we have central heating and sitting-rooms, the game has lost some of the charm it must have had when Victoria was Queen. A white sheet is hung across the room and a light shone on to it. The players divide into two teams, and members of one team take it in turns to walk across the room behind the sheet so that their shadows are thrown on to it. The opposing team sits in front guessing who it is who is going by. Obviously, the shadow players must do all they can to disguise their silhouettes. After each member of the first team has crossed the room at least twice, the teams swap round. At the end of the game, the team with the most correct guesses wins.

OVER THE STICKS △

Players: *any number*
Equipment: *half as many chairs as players and two blindfolds*

Upright chairs are arranged in two facing rows down the centre of the room leaving a narrow passageway between them. Half the party sit on the chairs so their feet are just touching, and the other half leave the room. Two of the players from outside are brought back in and are made to stand at one end of the line of chairs. They are allowed to look at the positions of the feet of the people who are sitting down, and then they are blindfolded. They are then instructed to walk down the line, taking care to step over the feet of those sitting there. Just as they are setting off on their journey, the seated guests silently draw in their feet, so that the couple walk down the line carefully trying to avoid something that isn't there. When they have got to the end of the line and are congratulating themselves on their dextrous navigation, they are unmasked. By this time the seated guests must have their feet out again. Two more players are brought in and (perhaps) fooled in the same way. Only when most of the outsiders have had a go is the deception explained (unless it is discovered by accident!).

UP JENKINS △

Players: *six, eight or ten*
Equipment: *chairs for all players, a table, a coin*

This is a light-hearted game of observation and deduction, which offers plenty of scope for bluffing and general merriment.

The players are divided into two equal teams and seated on opposite sides of the table. If the table is small, and the players squashed together, this adds to the fun. Members of one team pass the coin from hand to hand below the table. When the leader of the opposing team calls 'Up Jenkins,' the players on the team with the coin raise their hands, with fists clenched, well above the table. One fist, of course, will be concealing the coin. The leader of the opposing team then calls 'Down Jenkins' and the raised hands must be slapped down on the table with palms flat.

The opposing team now have to guess which hand the coin is under. The leader confers with his team-mates and then taps the hand that they think conceals the coin. The hand is raised, and if the coin is revealed the guessing team scores a point, otherwise the team with the coin scores a point.

The teams change roles for the next round. The winners are the team with the greatest number of points when an agreed number of rounds have been played.

The game may also be played so that the guessing team is allowed three guesses to discover the hand concealing the coin, scoring three points if their first guess is correct, two points if their second guess is correct, and one point if their third guess is correct.

PAN-TAPPING △

Players: *two, plus audience*
Equipment: *a saucepan and a wooden spoon*

One player is sent out of the room, while the others decide on something they want him to do on his return. It might be to peel a grape, to turn a somersault, or kiss the woman everyone knows he has been wanting to kiss for years. When the player is brought back into the room, another player guides his actions by beating on the bottom of a saucepan with a wooden spoon. When the outsider moves towards the object he has to touch, or towards a position in which he has to perform the desired action, the pan-tapper beats loudly upon his or her instrument. When the player moves away from his objectives, the pan-tapper beats more softly. The nearer the player comes to the objective the louder the pan-tapper beats, until either the player has done what he has to do or the pan-tapper's wrists have collapsed. If the player does have to kiss someone, it is usually more amusing to make him kiss something less predictable than a lip. The nape of the neck, the ear lobe, the back of the knees, are all neglected erogenous zones towards which a talented pan-tapper can lead an eager outsider with great effect.

ROYAL COURT △

Players: *any even number*
Equipment: *a pack of cards*

It's no use suggesting a Romping Game to a sober-suited bunch of obvious bridge players. The subtle host or hostess must seduce them into the romp by asking them if they fancy a novel card game. Having established that the guests would enjoy nothing more, the host or hostess – assuming for the moment there are sixteen players – takes a pack of cards, sorts out the ace, king, queen and jack of all four suits and places them face-down on the floor. Each player then has to rush forward and pick up a card. Those who pick up the aces are the leaders of their suits and, calling out the name of their suit, they make for the nearest empty chair and sit on it. The other three players with cards of the same suit run towards their leader. The king sits on the ace's lap, the queen on the king's lap, and the jack on the queen's lap. The first four players to get in this position win. With just one pack of cards the game can accommodate up to fifty-two players in four courts of thirteen, and the more very much the merrier. The game may not be as complex as bridge, but it's *kinder*. And in this world that counts for a lot.

SARDINES △ △

Players: *any even number*
Equipment: *none*

Queen Victoria played this game. So did most of her subjects. It is one of the most popular parlour games the world has known, and anyone who hasn't played it has hardly lived. All the guests assemble in one room and remain there for two or three minutes while a selected couple go forth quietly to hide themselves together somewhere – *anywhere* – in the house. At the end of the two or three minutes the other guests set out in pairs to search for the hidden couple, and the first pair to locate them in their hideaway must join them there. As each succeeding pair discovers the hideaway, they too must join the occupants – but silently. If twenty-six students from the City of London College can perch together on top of a pillar box in Finsbury Circus, Sardines players should have little difficulty packing themselves into roomy larders, loos and wardrobes, or under double beds. (Note to host and hostess: if you are intending to play this game, vacuum under the beds before the guests arrive.) The game can be given added spice by requiring the pairs to adopt the *exact pose* of the original couple when they find them.

WITCH HUNT △ △

Players: *any number*
Equipment: *a black cloak and black pointed hat, if available*

Adults who think Hide and Seek is juvenile consider Witch Hunt to be the height of sophistication. In fact, it is just Hide and Seek in witch's clothing. The witch-hunters gather in the darkened bathroom or kitchen, while the witch goes through the house turning off all the lights and finding him- or herself a suitable spot in which to hide. After five tense, spook-laden minutes, the witch-hunters emerge and set out to find the witch. It they call out, 'Where are you, Witchy?' the witch must answer with an appropriately eerie cackle. The witch may move about as he or she pleases. Whoever succeeds in catching the witch becomes the witch for the next round. The game can be given an authentic flavour if the person playing the witch is given a black cloak and a pointed hat to wear. There is a college professor in Maryland, USA, who when playing the game provides the witch with a complete sorcerer's costume, and dresses all the witch-hunters in the garb of the Ku Klux Klan.

Word Games

I Spy
Ad Infinitum
Spelling Bee
Backward Spelling
Adverbial Answers
Botticelli
Last and First
Fizz, Buzz, Fizz-Buzz
Initial Answers
Word Associations
Number Associations.
Twenty Questions
Character Assassination
Donkey
Traveller's Alphabet
Fame and Fortune
Initials
Portmanteau
The Moulting Ostrich
Pandora's Box
Obliquity
What Nonsense!
Stepping Stones
Proverbs
Coffee Pot
Taboo
Yes and No
Why? When? How? Where?
Famous Last Words

I SPY △ △

Players: *any number*
Equipment: *none*

It may be a simple game that everybody has played, but it is none the less popular for that. One player thinks of some object that is visible in the room – a spoon, for example – and announces to the other players its initial letter, saying, 'I spy with my little eye something beginning with S.' The other players then have to guess what the object is. 'Sideboard?' 'Shoe?' 'Ceiling???' 'Scissors?' and so on. The first player to guess correctly 'spies' the next object.

AD INFINITUM ⌒♫

Players: *any number*
Equipment: *a stop-watch*

This game requires a judge equipped with a stop-watch to monitor the proceedings. The players sit on the floor in a circle with their knees touching (or intertwined, depending on the mood and agility of the parties involved) and tell a story. Each player must talk for thirty seconds without hesitating or repeating himself, and at the end of thirty seconds the next player must immediately pick up the story and continue it, without ever bringing it to a conclusion. Anyone who pauses, repeats himself, or apparently ends the story, is out. The last person left talking is the winner and, as a reward, can end the story in any way he or she wants.

The judge must decide when a pause is not a pause, a repetition not a repetition, and an ending not an ending. He or she must also time the thirty seconds fairly and accurately. The judge may also choose a title for the story, and pick the player who starts it.

SPELLING BEE △

Players: *any number*
Equipment: *none*

One player acts as question master and calls out a word to each of the other players in turn, who must then give the correct spelling of the word. If the player spells the word correctly he or she scores one point.

The question master may call the words from a prepared list or may make up the list as he or she goes along. Words should be chosen to suit the abilities of the players. When a predetermined number of rounds have been played, the player with the greatest number of points is the winner.

The game may also be played in the following variations:

1. It is played as described above, except that a player who fails to spell a word correctly drops out. The winner is the last player left in.

2. A player who spells a word correctly is given another word to spell. If he or she spells that correctly, another is given, and so on. A point is scored for each correct spelling, and the player's turn ends only when he or she fails to spell a word correctly. The player with the most points at the end of the game is the winner.

3. The players are divided into two teams, sitting opposite each other. The question master calls out a word to each player in turn, selecting the two teams alternately. A player who spells a word correctly scores a point for the team, but if the word is mis-spelt, it is offered to his or her opposite number in the other team. If this player spells it correctly, he or she scores a bonus point for the team.

BACKWARD SPELLING 🎓

Players: *any number*
Equipment: *none*

This is a form of Spelling Bee which is made more difficult because the words have to be spelled backwards. It can be played in any of the ways described for Spelling Bee.

ADVERBIAL ANSWERS 🎓

Players: *any number*
Equipment: *pieces of paper for each guest*

Before the guests arrive, the host or hostess must jot down a number of unlikely adverbs on scraps of paper, as many as there are guests. When the guests arrive, each is given his or her adverb, and must spend the evening talking in the manner prescribed. This can be great fun for those given 'saucily' or 'tenderly', but can be rough on those who get 'flabbily', 'superciliously' or 'repulsively'. At the end of the evening, or when the host or hostess – who have probably given themselves 'enchantingly' and 'delightfully' – feel that everyone has had enough, the guests gather round and try to guess each other's adverbs.

BOTTICELLI 🎓 ✿

Players: *any number*
Equipment: *none*

One player thinks of the name of a famous person or fictitious character and reveals the first letter of his or her subject's surname to the company, who then fire a series of indirect questions at him or her. When the player is unable to answer them correctly, the questioners may elicit a clue as to the identity of the thought-of personage by asking a direct question, requiring a Yes or No answer. Suppose Adam thinks of Botticelli (the fifteenth-century painter who kindly, if posthumously, lent his name to the game), he reveals to the others that his character is 'someone beginning with B'. They will then ask him indirect questions, such as, 'Are you a German composer?' or 'Are you an English writer?' to which he should reply, 'No, I am not Bach,' or 'No, I am not Bunyan.' However, if he can't think of the name of a German composer beginning with B, nor even of an English author, the questioners will cry, 'You fool, what about Bach?' or 'What about Bunyan?' and claim the right to ask a direct question about the unknown person, such as, 'Were you born before 1700?' or 'Are you male?'

The questioners must try to ask awkward indirect questions – to which, of course, they themselves must always have an answer – in the hope of gaining as many opportunities as possible to put the direct questions which should lead them to their answer.

So when, as a result of a dozen or more direct questions, it has been established that Adam is, in fact, a male Italian artist born before 1500, it may occur to one of the questioners that Adam is Botticelli. If it does, he or she may not put the direct question 'Are you Botticelli?' unless they have earned the right to a direct question in the usual way. The player can, however, put an indirect question, such as, 'Were you the man who painted the *Birth of Venus* and had a number of works burnt by Savonarola?' in which case poor Adam has no alternative but to reply, 'Yes, I am Botticelli.'

Players who choose to be William Shakespeare, the Princess of Wales and Margaret Thatcher tend to be discovered almost at once. Players choosing to be Peter Pan, God, or the host or hostess, tend to have a pleasantly long innings.

LAST AND FIRST △

Players: *any number*
Equipment: *none*

A category is chosen – Birds, Cities, Rivers, TV Programmes,

Comedians – or whatever. The first player calls out any word belonging to the chosen category. The second player calls out another, beginning with the last letter of the first word. The next player calls out another, beginning with the last letter of the previous word, and so on. For example, if the chosen category were Animals, the words might be: dog, gorilla, anteater, rabbit, tiger, rat, toad and so on.

All the words called out must belong to the chosen category and no word may be repeated. Any player who fails to think of a word, or calls out a word which does not belong to the category, or which has already been used, must drop out of the game. The last player left in is the winner.

FIZZ, BUZZ, FIZZ-BUZZ △

Players: *any number*
Equipment: *none*

Fizz, Buzz and Fizz-Buzz are three closely related games, and they are all very silly. For any of the three games the players sit or stand in a circle and call out numbers, one after the other. The first player calls out, 'One' the second, 'Two,' the third, 'Three,' and so on round the circle, as quickly as possible.

If Fizz is being played, then the word 'Fizz' must be substituted for every multiple of 5, and substituted for the digit 5 whenever it occurs in a number. Thus 5, 10 and 15 should all be pronounced 'Fizz', and 50 and 51 should be pronounced 'Fizzty' and 'Fizzty-one'.

Buzz is similar, except that 7 is the forbidden number, and the word 'Buzz' is substituted for it.

Fizz-Buzz (believe it or not) is a combination of Fizz and Buzz. Thus 75 is 'Buzzty-Fizz' and 57 becomes 'Fizzty-Buzz'.

You may, if you wish, switch from Fizz to Buzz to Fizz-Buzz in the course of a game, just to make it more confusing.

Any player who says a number instead of fizzing (or vice versa), or who fizzes when they should have buzzed (or vice versa) drops out of the game. The last player left in is the winner.

INITIAL ANSWERS △

Players: *any number*
Equipment: *none*

One player is chosen to be the questioner for the first round. He or she asks any appropriate question, which must be answered by each of the other players in turn. Each player's answer must consist of words beginning with his or her own initials. For example, to the question, 'What kind of food do you like?', Clive James might reply 'Cherry jam', Stephanie Beacham might reply, 'Spaghetti bolognese', Lenny Henry might reply, 'Lean ham', and Zsa Zsa Gabor might decide she did not want to play the game after all. A player who fails to give a satisfactory answer within five seconds becomes the questioner for the next round.

WORD ASSOCIATIONS △

Players: *any number*
Equipment: *none*

The players sit or stand in a circle. The first player says the first word that comes into his or her mind. The second player immediately says the first word that comes into his or her mind in response to the first player's word. The third player responds likewise to the second player's word, and so on round and round the circle. If a player hesitates before saying a word he or she is out. The last player left in is the winner. This game is sometimes called Psychotherapy, and psychiatrists charge high fees for playing it with you.

NUMBER ASSOCIATIONS 🐾🐟

Players: *any number*
Equipment: *none*

Each player in turn calls out any number between 1 and 12. Whoever is first among the other players to respond with an appropriate association scores a point. For example, the number 2 might prompt the associations, 'A Tale of Two Cities', 'In two ticks', 'Tea for Two', and so on. The number 5 might prompt 'Five Star', 'Five-finger exercise', 'Five stones', etc. No association may be repeated. The player with the greatest number of points when everyone has had enough of the game is the winner.

TWENTY QUESTIONS 🐟

Players: *any number*
Equipment: *none*

Thanks to the radio, this became one of the most famous word games in the world. Played at home, all an individual has to do is to think of an object and inform the company whether it is animal, vegetable, mineral, abstract, or a bit of each. The others then fire questions, requiring only Yes or No answers, and designed to limit the field and eventually close in on the object. Each player takes a turn at thinking of an object and is the winner if the other players have not discovered the object after asking a maximum of twenty questions.

CHARACTER ASSASSINATION 🐟 ☠ 🍷

Players: *four or more*
Equipment: *none*

There is nothing quite like this unpleasant game for boosting morale among the people who play it. It is ideal for bringing back colour to the cheeks of the wan and weary. Players divide into two teams. Team A secretly selects a person to slander and proceeds to do just that – without actually mentioning their victim's name – for the benefit of Team B, who must guess the identity of the maligned individual as quickly as they can. When Team B has guessed Team A's victim, it is Team B's own turn to run someone down. The team that guesses the other team's victim in the shorter space of time, wins.

However malicious – or drunk – the players happen to be, it is best to denigrate only public figures. A player who lays into his host or hostess, or his own mother-in-law, is liable to say things he may later regret. And assassinating the character of a player who is present is needlessly cruel, even if that player appears prepared to run him- or herself down.

DONKEY 🖎

Players: *any number*
Equipment: *a dictionary*

This is a spelling game, in which the players must build words but never finish them. If Adam and Eve were playing, Adam might begin with an 'A' (for 'apple') and Eve might add a 'C' (for 'actor'); Adam could follow that with a 'T' (ending a three-letter word doesn't count) and Eve might continue with an 'I' (thinking now of 'actinal' which would end on Adam), only to be countered by an 'O' from Adam which would leave her with no alternative but to say 'N' making 'action', and losing one of her six lives by ending a word. Players cannot pick letters at random. They must be thinking of a specific word when they say a letter, and if their opponents don't believe they are spelling a real word, they can challenge them. If the dictionary upholds the word, the challenger loses a life. If the word does not appear to have occurred to the compilers of the dictionary, the challenged individual loses a life. The last person to become a donkey – and donkeys are players who have lost all six lives – is the winner.

For what it's worth, and for whoever can manage to remember it, the longest word in the English language is 'floccinaucinihili-

71

'pilification', meaning (somewhat significantly) 'the action of estimating as worthless'.

TRAVELLER'S ALPHABET △

Players: *any number*
Equipment: *none*

This is an alphabet sequence game. The players sit in a circle, and each asks the player on his or her left two questions: 'Where are you going?' and 'What will you do when you get there?' The replies consist of the name of a country and the description of an activity, using verb, adjective and noun, all beginning with the same letter. The first player's replies must begin with the letter A, the second's with the letter B, the third with the letter C, and so on. The conversation might go like this:

> Adam: 'Where are you going?'
> Eve: 'To Austria.'
> Adam: 'What will you do when you get there?'
> Eve: 'Appreciate Austrian apples.'
> Eve: 'Where are you going?'
> Cain: 'To Barbados.'
> Eve: 'What will you do when you get there?'
> Cain: 'Baffle Barbadian babies.'
> Cain: 'Where are you going?'
> Abel: 'To Canada.'
> Cain: 'What will you do when you get there?'
> Abel: 'Collect carved camels.'

Any player who fails to reply within a reasonable time limit drops out of the game. The winner is the last person left in.

FAME AND FORTUNE 🖎

Players: *any number*
Equipment: *sweets, nuts, or whatever as prizes*

The host or hostess announces a number of categories – Deceitful Politician, International Criminal, Atrocious Actor, Boring Novelist, and the like – and the guests must call out names which fit the bill. The player judged to have called out the most appropriate name first in each category gets a prize – a peanut or a raspberry jujube. When all the categories have been gone through, the player with the most peanuts or jujubes wins a more substantial prize – a sack of nuts *and* a bag of jujubes.

INITIALS 🖎

Players: *any number*
Equipment: *none*

Each player in turn calls out any pair, trio or quartet of initials that occur to them and the first competitor to come up with a suitable, and authentic meaning, scores a point. (Some initials stand for more than one meaning, so a dictionary might be useful.) AA, BBC, RIP and the like are predictable and make the game too easy to be fun. But combinations like AIA, DAQMG, TVA and FANY offer a much greater challenge, and the players who come back, quick as a flash, with Associate of the Institute of Actuaries, Deputy Assistant Quarter-Master General, Tennessee Valley Authority and First Aid Nursing Yeomanry, deserve all the points they get.

PORTMANTEAU 📖

Players: *any number*
Equipment: *none*

This is a memory game, in which players have to remember an ever-lengthening list of odd items. The first player begins by saying, 'I packed my portmanteau and in it I put *The Book of Common Prayer*.' The second player then says, 'I packed my portmanteau and in it I put *The Book of Common Prayer* and my purple and yellow striped Marks and Spencer's knickers.' The third player continues, 'I packed my portmanteau and in it I put *The Book of Common Prayer*, my purple and yellow striped Marks and Spencer's knickers and my yellow nightie which Aunt Agatha gave me for my birthday last year.' And so it goes on around the group, until somebody forgets an item or gets an item in the wrong order. (Obviously the longer and more complicated the descriptions of the items are, the more difficult the game becomes.) The faltering and forgetful drop out and the others continue to pack their portmanteaux until all but the victor have fallen by the wayside.

THE MOULTING OSTRICH △ △

Players: *any number*
Equipment: *none*

A leader is chosen, and all he or she has to do is to make the other players smile or laugh. Grinning himself, he says to each player in turn, 'Alas, alas, lackaday, my poor ostrich is moulting and I don't know what to do.' To this, each player must make a reasonable suggestion, keeping a totally straight face all the while. Anyone caught smiling, smirking, giggling or bursting into wild hysterics is disqualified.

When the leader goes into the second round he or she adds another problem. He or she might say, 'Alas, alas, lackaday, my poor ostrich is moulting and I've got a boil and can't sit down and I don't know what to do.' Again, each player must make, poker-faced, a reasonable, helpful suggestion. For the third round, the leader might say, 'Alas, alas, lackaday, my poor ostrich is moulting and I've got a boil and can't sit down and my mother-in-law exploded in church last Sunday and I don't know what to do.' Any player surviving all three rounds is a winner.

PANDORA'S BOX

Players: *any number*
Equipment: *a box or chest filled with assorted objects; cards bearing the names of each guest*

Before the party the box or chest is filled with an eccentric collection of objects, for example, a dog collar (human or canine), a Christmas cracker, a copy of *Spycatcher*, an egg, a toupee, a bra, a love letter, a stocking with a hole in it, a knitting needle, a pineapple, a marble, a soup ladle, and cards bearing the names of the guests. The guests gather round the hamper and each in turn, with eyes closed, picks three objects and two cards from it. He or she then has to tell a story involving the objects and the guests named on the cards. The more outrageous the objects, the more outrageous the story. The winner is the player whose tale is judged the most intriguing.

OBLIQUITY

Players: *any number*
Equipment: *none*

Players take it in turns to mention the names of famous people in the most oblique of associated forms. 'Smooth Sagittarian' would be Jeffrey Archer (remember the back?), 'Antipodean Apollo' would be Rupert Murdoch (*Sun* god), 'That's dentistry' would be Esther Rantzen (an easy one, that). The other players are allowed to ask three questions requiring only Yes or No answers before making a guess as to the identity of the obliquely named individual. Then, if they don't track down the hidden name in three guesses, a point goes to the inventor. The player with the most points wins.

WHAT NONSENSE!

Players: *three or more*
Equipment: *as many pieces of paper as there are players, and a pencil*

This game requires a little preparation, for it requires the devising of a list of topics – as many as there are players – on which players have to talk a lot of nonsense for two minutes. Each topic is written on a slip of paper, which is then folded and dropped into a hat, or similar container. Each player picks a slip at random, and then has to speak his or her nonsense. The player judged to have attained the highest peaks of lunacy wins.

Suitably daft topics might be:

1. Teaching goldfish to talk.
2. Composing sonatas on a computer.
3. New uses for old toothpaste tubes.
4. Teaching the blind to drive.
5. How to give a party on the seabed.
6. Who *did* kill Cock Robin?

Or you might like to delve into the realm of metaphysics:

7. The answer that cannot be questioned.
8. Which came first, the chicken or the egg?
9. Man's position in time and space.
10. The functionalism of inverse dichotomy.

STEPPING STONES 🖎

Players: *between two and eight*
Equipment: *pencils and paper might be necessary*

This is a mentally stimulating game of word associations, which may be played on any level from the banal to the esoteric. Each player in turn is given five themes by the other players. For example, a player might be told to get from Animals to Travel, via Cookery, Art and Fashion. He or she may use up to nine statements or phrases as stepping stones, and must touch on each of the themes in the order given. The other players must satisfy themselves that all the themes have been covered, that the sequence of associations is valid, and that any allusions, puns or jokes are not too far-fetched.

Here is one way in which the example above might work out:

1. A sheep is a very useful animal to man. (Animals)
2. Its meat is used to make hotpot. (Cookery)
3. Hotpot is cooked in a large earthenware dish.
4. Earthenware dishes and jugs often feature in still-life paintings. (Art)
5. Artists like Gainsborough painted portraits of ladies wearing the latest fashionable gowns. (Fashion)
6. A fashionable gown is very useful when travelling to glamorous foreign cities like Paris and Rome. (Travel)

PROVERBS 🖎

Players: *any number*
Equipment: *none*

It says in *The Book of Proverbs* that 'A merry heart maketh a cheerful countenance'. And this game, played regularly at Osborne House in Queen Victoria's time, has been the cause of many happy hearts and faces. One player leaves the room while the remainder think of a well-known proverb, such as 'A stitch in time saves nine'. The outsider then returns and puts a question –

any question, about anything under the sun – to each of the players in turn. The first person to answer uses the first word of the proverb in his or her reply, the second uses the second word, and so on. By the time all the players have answered two questions, the outsider has to guess the proverb, by which time he or she may have heard it once, twice, or three and three-quarter times, depending on the number of words in the proverb and players in the game.

COFFEE POT ⤳

Players: *between three and eight*
Equipment: *none*

People who are good at puns are good at playing Coffee Pot. One player thinks of a word which has two meanings, such as 'duck', or a pair of words which have different meanings but which sound the same, such as 'flower' and 'flour'. The player then says aloud a sentence using both meanings, but substituting the words 'coffee pot' for both of them. For example, using the words suggested above: 'If you see a low-flying coffee pot you'd better coffee pot,' or 'I couldn't pick a coffee pot from the garden because my hands were covered in coffee pot.'

Each of the other players may then ask one question, and the first player's answer must include one or other of the chosen words, again disguised as 'coffee pot'. If one of the players manages to identify the 'coffee pot' he or she scores a point, otherwise the first player scores the point. Each player has a go at being a 'coffee potter', and the player who finishes with the greatest number of points is the winner.

TABOO 🕮

Players: *any number*
Equipment: *none*

One letter in the alphabet is taboo and must not be uttered. Once the host or hostess has announced it, he or she questions each player in turn, and the player must reply without using any word containing the forbidden letter. Any player who does use the taboo letter drops out. The last player left answering the questions wins.

YES AND NO 🕮

Players: *any even number*
Equipment: *five pennies for each player*

Players, equipped by a magnanimous host with five pennies apiece, pair off. They ask one another questions, and whoever is tricked into saying Yes or No in the course of the conversation is presented with a penny. The first player to get rid of his five pennies wins. An alternative, and good getting-to-know-you, way of playing the game involves players moving on to a new partner every time they give away or have to accept a penny.

WHY? WHEN? HOW? WHERE? 🕮

Players: *any number*
Equipment: *none*

One player is sent from the room, while the others agree on an object or an individual for them to identify on their return. When the player does return, he or she must ask each person in turn, 'Why do you like it?' The players must reply sensibly, but without divulging the actual identity of the chosen person or thing. Suppose the 'object' chosen were 'cricket'. The answer to the question might be, 'Because it is peaceful.' Then, to the second question, 'When do you like it?' the answer might be, 'Every Saturday afternoon.' The third question, 'How do you like it?' might be answered by, 'Fast and furious.' And the last question, 'Where do you like it?' might be answered by 'On a village green.' During this questioning the outsider must try to guess the object's identity, and when he or she has put the four questions to the company, he or she is allowed three guesses. Players take it in turns to leave the room.

FAMOUS LAST WORDS 🎓

Players: *any number*
Equipment: *none*

The players sit in a circle and simply invent the 'famous last words' of anyone they care to think of, be they dead or dying – which includes just about everybody. It's no use offering, 'Die, my dear doctor, that's the last thing I'll do!' as Palmerston's last words because those *were* his last words. Only original exit lines will do. The Russian film writer and producer Monja Danischewsky, who devised the game, claimed his favourite was the famous last words of the Fatted Calf: 'I hear the young master has returned.'

Pencil and Paper Games

AA
Consequences Mark I
Consequences Mark II
Beetle
Hangman
Memory Hangman
Boxes
The Worm
Famous Names
Feelers
Noises Off
Harsh Sentence
Sprouts
Categories
Observation
Wordbuilder
Combinations
Anagrams
Scaffold
Picasso
Advertisements
Pig's Tail
Royal Academy
Short Story
Crosswords
Taste Buds
Who's This?

AA 🖎

Players: *any number*
Equipment: *paper and pencil for each player*

Some sad individuals, either because of a deprived childhood or a mistaken sense of intellectual superiority, tend to deprecate party games. As soon as the host dons a party hat and starts talking about Charades, the games-hater looks at his watch and announces it's time he was leaving. Obviously there is no point in forcing a reluctant guest into a riotous game of Blind Man's Buff, but it is worth coaxing him into something more gentle and, ostensibly, more cerebral. AA has nothing to do with automobiles, alcoholics, accountants, architects or amateur athletics. It is simply a paper and pencil challenge which few can resist.

Each player is invited to write down a letter of the alphabet – any letter will do. Then the host explains that each player must write down a brief anecdote, short story, scenario, biography or verse in which every word begins with the letter the player put at the top of the paper. Ten minutes are allowed, at the end of which the players must read out their efforts and elect a winner.

CONSEQUENCES MARK I 🖎 ♉

Players: *any number*
Equipment: *paper and pencil for each player*

Characters in Agatha Christie's novels don't play Consequences, but one feels they ought to, because it is the archetypal country-house parlour game. Each player is given a long sheet of paper and a pencil and told to write down certain information. Each time the player has written down the information, he or she folds the top of the paper forwards to cover what has been written and passes the folded sheet to the player on his or her right, while at the same time receiving a different folded sheet from the player on his or her left. So each player is adding fresh information to every sheet of paper, without any knowledge of what has been written previously. The pieces of information build up into a story, or, rather, as many stories as there are players, and the stories are read aloud at the end of the game. The thirteen pieces of information which must be written down are:

1. An adjective describing a person's appearance or character. (Fold paper and pass on.)
2. The name of a girl or woman – real, fictitious, alive or dead. (Fold paper and pass on.)
3. The word 'met' and an adjective describing another person's appearance or character. (Fold paper and pass on.)
4. The name of a man – real, fictitious, alive or dead. (Fold paper and pass on.)
5. The word 'at' and the place where the girl met the man. (Fold paper and pass on.)
6. The circumstances under which they met. (Fold paper and pass on.)
7. When they met. (Fold paper and pass on.)
8. The words, 'He said to her', together with whatever he said. (Fold paper and pass on.)
9. The words, 'And she replied', together with whatever she said. (Fold paper and pass on.)
10. What he did then. (Fold paper and pass on.)
11. What she did then. (Fold paper and pass on.)
12. The words, 'And the consequence was', with details of the consequence. (Fold paper and pass on.)
13. The words, 'And the moral of the tale is', together with whatever it happens to be.

The result might be something like this:

Bombastic
Princess Anne
met
Innocent
Arthur Daley
at
Greenham Common
They met for tea

83

on January 1st
He said to her 'Small is beautiful.'
And she replied 'I prefer a melon.' He then got hiccups
She then switched on the television
And the consequence was
They got picked up by the police
And the moral of the tale is
Never go out without checking on your knicker elastic.

CONSEQUENCES MARK II △

Players: *any number*
Equipment: *paper and pencil for each player*

This is a simpler version of the same game, providing almost as much inconsequential humour but being less intellectually demanding, as it involves drawing, not writing. On their papers the players draw a full-length portrait, of a human or animal (or both), bit by bit, like this:

1. The hat. (Fold paper and pass on.)
2. The head. (Fold paper and pass on.)
3. The neck and neck apparel. (Fold paper and pass on.)
4. The torso, plus arms or wings. (Fold paper and pass on.)
5. From the hips to the knees. (Fold paper and pass on.)
6. From the knees to the ankles. (Fold paper and pass on.)
7. The feet.

BEETLE △

Players: *from two to six*
Equipment: *one die, plus paper and pencil for each player*

Beetle is the most popular family dice game – once so popular that specially printed cards were available for playing it, and people used to hold Beetle Drives. The objective of the game is to be the first person to complete a drawing of a beetle, step by step according to the throws of the die. No artistic ability is needed!

The beetle consists of thirteen parts: body, head, tail, two eyes, two feelers and six legs. The throws of the die required before a player can draw the specific parts of the body are:

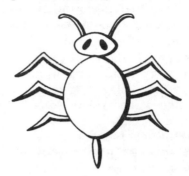

1 for the body
2 for the head
3 for each leg
4 for each eye
5 for each feeler
6 for the tail

A player has to throw a 1 before he or she can start, as the body must be drawn first. Similarly, the eyes and feelers cannot be added until the head has been drawn. The players take it in turn to throw the die, with each player throwing it once only in each round.

The first player to complete his or her beetle wins the round, but the game can be played on an aggregate of points. A round ends when one player has completed the beetle and thus scored thirteen points, one for each part of its body. The other players tot up how many parts they have drawn, and therefore how many points they have gained. Further rounds are played, and the game is won by the first player to score 51 points.

HANGMAN 📖

Players: *two*
Equipment: *pencil and paper*

Each player in turn thinks of a six- or seven-letter word, which he or she writes down in dashes, adding two letters in their correct places to give a clue as to the word's identity. For example, RHUBARB might be written like this: R – – – – R – or like this: – – U B – – – . The opponent then tries to guess the other letters one by one, indicating the position and suggesting a letter to fit in. If they choose the right letter for the right place, the first player has to write it in. If, however, they choose wrongly, the first player starts to construct a gallows and a corpse, bit by bit, as shown in the illustration. The guessing player thus has eleven chances, before he has lost his round and been hanged. If the wordsmith wins, he or she scores a point, if the guessing player avoids being hanged, he or she wins and scores a point. They swap roles for the next round, and the player with the greatest number of points after an agreed number of rounds is the overall winner.

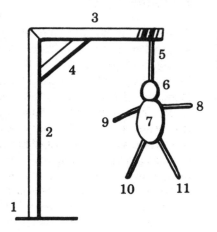

MEMORY HANGMAN

Players: *any number*
Equipment: *pencil and paper*

The players divide into two teams, and the leader of Team A announces that they have chosen a word of so many letters – say ten, if the word is REVOLUTION. The members of Team B then suggest letters which might be contained in the mystery word. If they are right, they are told the position of the letters in the word; if they are wrong, the leader of Team A starts to construct a gallows in the same way as in the previous game. No one, except the hangman himself, is allowed to write anything down.

The game is a memory test, and inveterate cheats should steer clear of it. The teams score points for winning as in the previous game.

BOXES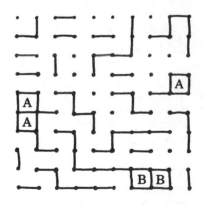

Players: *two*
Equipment: *paper and two pencils*

A square is constructed of ten rows of dots horizontally and vertically, and the players take it in turn to draw a straight line connecting any two dots which are next to each other, either horizontally or vertically. Diagonal lines are not allowed. The objective of the game is to complete as many 'boxes' as possible, which is achieved by completing the fourth side of a square when the other three sides have already been drawn. Each player, therefore, tries to avoid drawing the third side of a box, because to do so gives the opponent the chance of completing one. When a player completes a box he or she initials it and gets to draw another line. The game ends when all the boxes have been completed, and the player with the greatest number wins.

In the example shown, the player next to go will be able to complete a box in the right-hand corner.

The length of the game can be varied by starting with a larger or smaller square. Another version of it is played so the winner is the person who completes fewer boxes than his or her opponent. In this version players avoid having to draw the fourth side of a box.

THE WORM △

Players: *two*
Equipment: *paper and two pencils*

This is a similar game to Boxes, except that the aim is to avoid completing a square. A large square composed of ten vertical and ten horizontal dots is constructed as in the previous game. The first player draws a horizontal or vertical line to join any two adjacent dots. Diagonal lines are not allowed. The second player then draws another line, connecting either end of the existing line vertically or horizontally to any adjacent dot. The players continue playing in this manner, drawing a line from either end of the existing line or 'worm' to any adjacent dot. The objective is to force the opponent into a position in which he or she has to draw a line which will join either end of the 'worm' back on itself, for if this happens the player has lost the game. In the example illustrated, the player whose turn it is is bound to lose, since no matter which end he or she plays it will join the worm back on to itself.

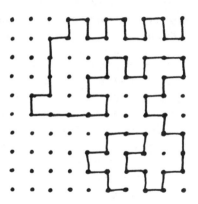

FAMOUS NAMES

Players: *any number*
Equipment: *pencil and paper for each player*

While the players sit poised with pencils at the ready, the host or hostess dictates to them a list of well-known surnames, which may come from fact or fiction, from characters alive or dead. The players then have two minutes in which to jot down the correct first name for each character. The surnames should not be made too obvious. A little imagination can provide a list that not only taxes the knowledge of the players, but also entertains them. For example, Rushdie, Tulliver, Scargill, Pavarotti, Betjeman and Oyl are the sort of surnames everyone will recognize, but which aren't always easy to fit first names to. If you put down Salman, Maggie, Arthur, Luciano, John and Olive, you would get full marks.

The game can be enlivened by providing surnames which might take several alternative first names. For Potter, do you put Beatrix or Dennis? For Murdoch, Rupert or Iris? For Fox, Charles James or Samantha? For Windsor, Elizabeth or Barbara? For Collins, Jackie, Joan or Sir William? In this version, players get three points for a first name no one else has thought of, two points for a name shared with others, and one point if all they can come up with is an initial. Incidentally, the world's commonest surname is not Smith, as many people believe, but Chang.

FEELERS △

Players: *any number*
Equipment: *pencil and paper for each player; a pillowcase, plus assorted odds and ends*

Fill the pillowcase with an assortment of strange objects, such as a large orange (which could be a grapefruit), a tenpence piece (which could be a twopence piece), a backscratcher (which could be a fork), a mug (which could be a cup), a whistle (which could be a cigarette lighter, a milk bottle (which could be a beer bottle), a yoyo (which could be anything) and so on, and pass the pillowcase around the players. Each has to feel it for thirty seconds and then write down a list of its supposed contents, and the player with the most accurate list wins. For the benefit of the psychic, include a book among the contents. Everyone will guess it is a book (though it *could* be a desk diary) but only those with very special gifts (or foreknowledge) will be able to supply its title.

NOISES OFF

Players: *any number*
Equipment: *pencil and paper for each player*

Behind a screen, or door, or the sofa, the host and hostess create a series of preposterous, outrageous and confusing noises, which the players must identify and jot down. The player who recognizes the sound of gargling, kissing, sandpaper on wood, the striking of a match, the bouncing of a ball, the cracking of an egg, the boiling of a kettle, the sucking of a lemon, the dropping of a pin, the clicking of fingers, and so on, wins.

HARSH SENTENCE

Players: *any number*
Equipment: *pencil and paper for each player*

Pick up a novel, a volume of verse, or even a newspaper, and write down the first word encountered which begins with the letter A, then the first that begins with B, and so on through the alphabet. Dictate the words to the players, who then have five minutes in which to construct an entertaining and intelligible sentence with them, using them in any order. The winner is the author of the sentence judged by the majority to be the best. The first few pages of Jane Austen's *Persuasion* offers: a, book, consolation, distressed, earliest, failed, Gloucester, has, issue, June, Kellynch, lord, more, never, or, promoted, quit, rather, silly, to, unreasonably, very, would – and you can excuse the X, Y and Z.

SPROUTS 🎓

Players: *two*
Equipment: *paper and two pencils*

The game begins with three, four or five dots being marked at random on a sheet of paper. Each player in turn draws a line beginning and ending on any of the dots, which may join two dots together or may loop round and end on the dot it started from, and then draws a new dot on the line just drawn. If four dots were started with, after both players have had a turn, the position might look like that in the first illustration.

In drawing the lines, these rules must be observed: no line may cross any other line or pass through a dot; no dot may have more than three lines leading from it. The players continue playing alternately until no more lines can be drawn, and the player who draws the last line is the winner. For example, in the second illustration, the player with the next turn will win. The only line which can be drawn will connect the top and bottom dots, and, even though a new dot will be created on that line, it will be impossible to draw any further lines.

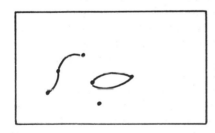
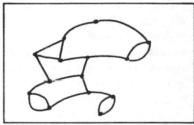

CATEGORIES 🎓

Players: *two or more*
Equipment: *paper and pencil for each player*

The players construct a list of categories, preferably twelve or more, which they write down. The categories may be simple, such as Animals, Birds, Items of Clothing, Food and Drink, etc., or more specialized, such as Peruvian Footballers, Hydrocarbons, People and Places Named in Proust's *A La Recherche du Temps Perdu*, depending on the kind of people who are playing the game. Then a letter of the alphabet is chosen at random, a time limit, of, say, ten minutes is agreed, and the players then have to write down as many words as they can for each category beginning with the chosen letter. When the time is up, each player reads out his or her list of words. A word which has not been thought of by any other player scores two points; a word which one or more players have also listed scores one point. The player with the greatest number of points wins. For subsequent rounds a new initial letter is chosen, and the categories may remain as they are, or changed.

A more complicated version of this game can be played by choosing a keyword of five or more letters instead of an initial letter. This keyword is written out across the top of the paper, and the categories are listed down the side. Players must then write down one word beginning with each letter of the keyword for each category. For example, if the keyword chosen were TEAMS, the list might look something like this:

	T	E	A	M	S
Animals	tortoise	elephant	aardvark	mouse	sheep
Birds	tern	egret	albatross	magpie	swift
Colours	turquoise	ebony	amber	mauve	sepia
Food	tagliatelle	egg	apple	mince pie	sugar

OBSERVATION

Players: *any even number*
Equipment: *pencil and paper for each player*

This is a sexist game, but none the less amusing for all that. The guests are divided into the sexes, and each man is told to go and talk to one woman for one minute. At the end of that time, the women are sent from the room, and each man has to write down a description of what the woman he was talking to was wearing.

The most detailed and accurate description wins. The roles are then reversed, and the women guests told to go and talk to a man for one minute. At the end of that time, the men are sent out of the room and each woman has to write down a description of what the man they were talking to said. Again, the most detailed and accurate account wins. The game could, of course, be played the other way round, with the men noting what the women said, and the women noting what the men wore.

WORDBUILDER

Players: *two or more*
Equipment: *paper and pencil for each player*

A starter word is chosen, preferably a long one, such as PHOTOGRAPHIC, and given to the players. They then have ten minutes in which to write down as many words as they can which can be made from the letters of the chosen word. The only rules are that each word must contain at least four letters; proper nouns are not allowed; foreign words, abbreviations and plurals are not allowed; a letter may only be used in a word as many times as it occurs in the starter word. A dictionary is helpful to check any disputed words. For example, supposing the chosen word were CONTRABAND, the following are some of the words which can be made from it:

Abandon, acorn, adorn, bacon, band, bard, barn, baron, brand, brat, broad, cant, card, cart, carton, cord, corn, crab, dart, road, toad, trod.

COMBINATIONS

Players: *two or more*
Equipment: *paper and pencil for each player*

A list of ten or more two- or three-letter combinations which can occur within words is prepared. For example, it might contain

letter combinations like this: – B L –   – B U L –   – G T H –   – I X –
– M N –   – M O N –   – Q U –   – R F –   – S U –   – T O G –

Each player writes down the list on his or her piece of paper, and then has five minutes in which to find as long a word as possible containing each of the letter combinations. They score one point per letter for each word, and the player with the highest total score wins.

Using the letter combinations listed above, a player might achieve a result like this:

TROUBLESOME	11 points
PERRFECTION	10
SIXTEENTH	9
STRENGTHEN	10
COMMONWEALTH	12
PREREQUISITE	12
CONDEMNED	9
PERSUASIVELY	12
EBULLIENCE	10
PHOTOGRAPHIC	12
Total =	107 points

ANAGRAMS

Players: *two or more (plus a question master)*
Equipment: *paper and pencil for each player*

The question master chooses a category, such as Countries, Rivers, Flowers, Cars, and prepares a list of words belonging in that category. He or she then makes an anagram of each word on the list, and gives each player a copy. The players are then given a time limit of five or ten minutes in which to unscramble the anagrams. The winner is the first player to unscramble all the words correctly, or the player with the greatest number of correct words when the time limit has expired.

For example, if the chosen category were Countries, the anagrams might include: REGALIA, AGALAMUTE, BEDRAUM,

WEDNES, COURADE and NETSETINCHILE, which would be unscrambled to form: Algeria, Guatemala, Bermuda, Sweden, Ecuador and Liechtenstein.

SCAFFOLD 🎓 🎓

Players: *two or more*
Equipment: *paper and pencil for each player*

The players are given the same three letters, such as R, D, T, and have ten minutes in which to form a list of words containing those three letters in the order given. Players score a point for each word listed, and the player with the highest score is the winner. For example, with the letters R, D, T, you might make Introduction, Credit, Product, Radiator, Predator and Graduate.

PICASSO 🎓

Players: *any even number*
Equipment: *paper and pencil for half the players, and an assortment of objects for the other half*

Pablo Picasso lent his name to this game because he once said: 'Painting is a blind man's profession. He paints not what he sees, but what he feels.' In this game, these words are taken literally. Players divide into pairs and each couple sits back to back. One half of the pair is given a pencil and paper and something to rest the paper on so he or she can write, and the other half is given an object. It could be a false moustache, a tube of toothpaste, a pomegranate, an egg whisk, or a carving knife. Without telling the partner what the object is, or anything about its use or associations, the player with it has to describe it to his or her partner, who has to draw it from the description. Anyone who turns up their nose at this game can be told that Picasso also said, 'Art is noble play.'

ADVERTISEMENTS 🕊

Players: *three or more*
Equipment: *old magazines, paper and pencils*

This game tests the players' powers of observation, and the advertising agencies' powers of persuasion. It requires a bit of preparation, for the photographs used to advertise well-known products have to be cut out of magazines, colour supplements and so on and either pasted on to a board or laid out on a table where the players can see them. Between ten and twenty photographs are enough, and they should be numbered to aid identification. The names of the products, logos or other tell-tale indications of where they come from must be removed before the players see them. Each player then has ten minutes in which to write down the names of the products being advertised. The player with the highest number of correct answers wins.

PIG'S TAIL 🛆 🍸

Players: *any number*
Equipment: *a blindfold and pencil for each player; a large drawing of a pig*

A huge tail-less pig is drawn on a huge sheet of paper which is pinned to a wall. One by one the players are blindfolded, handed a pencil, guided to the drawing and invited to draw the tail in the place they think is correct. The most accurately placed tail wins. A popular variation of the game involves the drawing of a caricature of a public figure we all love to hate – maybe Margaret Thatcher, Barry Manilow or Ian Paisley – and inviting the blindfolded players to add a demon's tail and horns, with the most aptly positioned taking the prize.

ROYAL ACADEMY

Players: *any even number*
Equipment: *two pencils and some paper*

This game is probably older than the Royal Academy of Arts, which was founded in 1768, and may well produce more exciting artistic efforts than the Academy's Summer Exhibition ever did. Be that as it may, the game is ideal for reviving a flagging party. The players divide into two teams, each of which clusters round a table or drawing board situated at opposite ends of the room. On the word, 'Go!' each team leader rushes to the host or hostess, who is sitting in the middle of the room, and who gives them, in a whisper, the same subject for a drawing. It might be something simple like the Mad Hatter's Tea Party or Oxford losing the Boat Race again, or it might be something esoteric or abstract, such as England engulfed by litter, or God sitting at the right hand of America. Equipped with their subjects, the team leaders rush back to their colleagues and start to draw the given scene. The team's members may make guesses at what is being drawn, but the artist can reply only by nodding or shaking the head. He or she may draw anything that might be helpful, but may not write any words. As soon as a correct guess is made – and the players may not blurt out their ideas loudly or their opponents will hear them – another member of the team darts off to the host or hostess to be given a fresh subject to draw. The first team to draw and guess all the scenes wins.

SHORT STORY

Players: *two or more*
Equipment: *pencil and paper for each player*

Within a set time limit of five or ten minutes, each player has to construct a short story, in which no word may be longer than three letters. When the time limit is up, the stories are read out and the player judged to have written the best story wins.

Here is an example of the kind of story that might be produced: A man had a pig in a sty, a cat and a hen. The cat ate the hen; the pig bit the man. The man was mad! He has no egg, but the pig is now ham.

CROSSWORDS 📖

Players: *two or more*
Equipment: *paper and pencil for each player*

Before the game begins, each player draws on his or her paper a grid with five squares across and five squares down. For a longer game, or for more than five players, a larger grid may be used. Each player calls out a letter of his or her choice, and all the players must then enter that letter in their grids, in any position they like. Once a letter has been entered it may not be removed. The aim is to form words with the letters, either across or down, and the game ends when all the squares have been filled in.

Scores are worked out according to the number of letters in the words each player has formed. Proper nouns, foreign words and abbreviations are not allowed, and one point is scored for each letter in a valid word. A letter may not be 'shared' in the score between two or more words in the same row or column. Thus a row reading CONET scores four points for CONE, but cannot also score points for CON, ON, ONE or NET. One bonus point is scored for each word that completely fills a row or column. The player with the highest score wins.

TASTE BUDS 📖

Players: *any number*
Equipment: *blindfolds, cups, and assorted liquids; pencil and paper for each player*

A number of cups – the plastic variety will do – are filled with a variety of different and distinctly flavoured liquids. The players are blindfolded, and take it in turns to sniff and sip the liquids, and note their guesses as to what they are. (If you are worried about hygiene, you could prepare a set of cups for each player.) Water, cold tea, cough mixture, gravy, lemon juice and so on are not difficult to recognize, but telling the difference between say, Bovril and Marmite, cocoa and drinking chocolate, London tap water and bottled spring water, Barsac and Sauternes, is rather more demanding and entertaining. The player with the most sensitive taste buds wins.

WHO'S THIS? △ △

Players: *any number*
Equipment: *paper and pencil for each player*

It has been said that a celebrity is someone who is known for being well known. For this game, the host or hostess collects lots of pictures of celebrities – cut out of newspapers or magazines, or real photographs. These are stuck on to a large sheet of paper or card and numbered, and the guests are given two, three or five minutes to jot down the names that fit the faces. The player with the longest correct list wins, and may be congratulated as being 'a natural celebrity spotter'.

Musical Games

Paul Jones
Musical Chairs Mark I
Musical Chairs Mark II
Grab
Musical Arches
Balloon Dance
Corpse Tango
Musical Reflexes
Musical Walking Stick
Musical Arms
Grand Chain
The Grand Old Duke of York
Musical Hats
Avoid-the-Hassock Dance
Musical Islands
O'Grady Sings
The Conductor
Pass the Parcel Mark I
Pass the Parcel Mark II
Musical Numbers
Musical Rush
Zounds Sounds

PAUL JONES △ △

Players: *any number*
Equipment: *a source of music*

This game is a variation of the classic ice-breaking dance which has been a traditional way of introducing guests who may not know each other for many years. The players form two circles, one inside the other, with the men on the outside facing inwards and the women on the inside facing outwards. When the music plays, the two circles dance round in opposite directions. When it stops, the men and women facing each other become partners, and must perform whatever task is set for them by the host or hostess, who calls out instructions, rather in the manner of a barn dance caller. The tasks should not be made too complicated or embarrassing for people who do not know each other well: a handshake, a pirouette, standing on one leg and hopping round in a circle, resting the hands on the partner's shoulders and jumping in the air – anything quick and lively, which will keep the game moving, is ideal. Start the music as soon as the pairs have finished, with the circles forming once more and moving in opposite directions. The game continues until most players have met each other. Obviously the person controlling the music should try to ensure that they stop it when different people are opposite each other.

MUSICAL CHAIRS MARK I △ △

Players: *eight or more*
Equipment: *a source of music; one chair fewer than there are players*

Whether you belong to the Mickey Mouse or the Roland Rat generation, as a child you *must* have played Musical Chairs. If you did, you will want to relive the pleasures of the game. If you didn't, you will want to find out what all the fuss is about.

Chairs, one fewer in number than the players, are placed in a circle, with the seats facing outwards. The players hold hands and dance round the ring to the music. As soon as the music stops, each player drops in to the nearest chair. The one failing to secure a chair drops out of the game, and removes one of the chairs. The player left dancing at the end wins.

MUSICAL CHAIRS MARK II △ △

Players: *eight or more*
Equipment: *a source of music; as many chairs as there are players*

The chairs are placed in a circle, one for each player, with the seats facing outwards. The players hold hands and dance round to sprightly music. As soon as the music stops, players scramble back to their own chairs – i.e. those they were standing by when the game started. The last person to get back to his or her chair when the music stops is obliged to sit in it for the rest of the game (so lazy players know what to aim for!), and must resist the temptation to trip up the remaining dancing players. The last player left dancing wins.

No party is complete without one of the two versions of Musical Chairs, but the game should always be played before a meal, because as a post-prandial romp it can be rough on the digestion.

GRAB △

Players: *any uneven number*
Equipment: *none*

This is an eighteenth-century game which has been unjustly neglected in recent years. All the players except one, who becomes the leader, choose partners and march nimbly round the room singing this traditional verse:

> *There was a jolly miller who lived by himself,*
> *As the wheel went round he made his wealth.*

One hand in the hopper, the other in the bag,
As the wheel went round he made a grab.

On the word 'grab', everyone must change partners and the leader attempts to grab a partner for him- or herself. After the skirmish, whoever is left without a partner becomes the lonely miller for the next round.

(The song is traditionally sung to an old folksong tune called 'Villikens and His Dinah', but if you are unacquainted with it, you can substitute a tune of your own.)

MUSICAL ARCHES △△

Players: *any even number*
Equipment: *a source of music*

This is an adult version of Oranges and Lemons, but without the song. Two pairs of players, one standing at each end of the room, join hands and raise them above their heads to form an arch. All the other players line up in pairs and dance through the two arches while the music plays. As soon as it stops the arches lower their arms to catch any pairs passing through. Any pair caught has to form another arch, and the game continues until every pair but one has been caught. The pair which remains is the winner. As many rounds of the game can be played as the players wish.

BALLOON DANCE △ ✿

Players: *any even number*
Equipment: *a source of music; a balloon for each player*

This is a very jolly and silly game, ideal for playing at Nursery Parties (guests are given jellies and jujubes to eat, and copies of *Dandy* and *Beano* to read), which are very popular. However, the game is a good one for any party, guaranteed to make it go with a swing.

The game is much like a Paul Jones, except that the dancers are obliged to hold balloons between their knees. The women form a circle in the middle facing outwards, and the men form an outer circle round them facing inwards. When the music plays, the circles perambulate in opposite directions, and when it stops each man asks the lady he is facing for a brief dance. Once this is over, the circles re-form and perambulate to music once again. Anyone bursting or dropping their balloon is eliminated, and anyone stranded without a partner when the music stops also drops out. The game can go on for as long as people like, or until there is only one couple left.

(*See also* Grand Chain, page 106.)

CORPSE TANGO △

Players: *any even number*
Equipment: *a source of music playing tango records*

The players tango until the music stops, when they have to 'freeze' instantly and completely in whatever position they happen to find themselves. The host and hostess then wander among them doing their utmost – by means of silly faces and even sillier remarks – to make the frozen figures twitch and snigger. They may not touch the players, and have only fifteen seconds in which to do their dirty work, when the music starts again, and the couples resume their tangoing. Any players caught moving once the music has stopped join the host and hostess in their attempt to get the corpses to betray signs of life. Play goes on in this way until only one victorious player remains.

MUSICAL REFLEXES △

Players: *any numbers*
Equipment: *a source of music*

One player (usually the host) operates the music with his back to the other players, but in full view of them. The other players face the operator's back, and sit on the floor, if they are young and active, or on chairs, if they are not. The operator switches on the music, and the other players have to judge when he is going to switch it off again, for when he does, they have to stand up. It is, of course, very difficult to judge exactly when the operator is going to switch off the music – some people get up too soon, and some too late – and it is made more difficult by the operator's exaggerated or trick movements, designed to confuse everyone.

The last one to rise before the music ends wins the round and gains one point. Anyone still sitting when the music ends loses a point. The first player to reach a total of five points is the overall winner, and operates the music in the next game.

MUSICAL WALKING STICK △

Players: *four or more*
Equipment: *a source of music and a walking stick*

If you don't have a walking stick, an umbrella or garden cane will do. The players sit on the floor, or on chairs, in a circle, and one of them is given the stick. The music is started, and the player with the stick is told to tap one end on the floor three times and then pass it to the player on their right. This player must also tap the stick three times before passing it on in a clockwise direction, with each player tapping the stick three times before parting with it. The player caught holding the stick when the music stops leaves the circle. This continues until only one player is left in the game, and he or she wins it.

MUSICAL ARMS △

Players: *eleven or more*
Equipment: *a source of music*

This game needs one more man than woman for one round; and one more woman than man for the next, so if the numbers are even, the odd one out can operate the music. For the first round, the men stand in line behind each other in the centre of the room. The first man stands with his right hand on his hip; the second player with his left hand on his hip; the third player with his right hand on his hip, and so on down the line. The women, numbering one more than the men, dance around the line as the music plays, and as soon as it stops, grab the arm of the nearest man. The one who fails to get an arm drops out, as does the first man in the queue. The game continues until there are just two vulture-like women left circling the last man, and the winner is the one who successfully grabs the final arm. The players then reverse roles, with the women standing in line with their arms half-akimbo, with one fewer man circling round them.

GRAND CHAIN △

Players: *any even number*
Equipment: *a balloon for each player; a source of music*

This good getting-to-know-you game involves every guest being given an inflated balloon as he or she arrives. The balloons should be of various colours, but there must be at least a pair of balloons of each colour. They are distributed at random, alternately to men and women, so that if a man guest gets a red balloon, then a lady guest, preferably not the one he came with, should also get a red balloon. The balloon partners must then seek each other out, and partner each other in the Grand Chain. Once all the guests have found themselves partners, they form a grand chain around the room, holding hands and holding their balloons between their knees. When the music starts the whole company troops round the room, moving in time with the music, which can be anything from a foxtrot to heavy metal rock. All those who drop or burst their balloon are eliminated, with their partners. Thus the game continues until all but the winning pair have left the chain.

THE GRAND OLD DUKE OF YORK △

Players: *eight or more*
Equipment: *none*

This classic children's party game is a very good one for warming up a party. You need a fair amount of space in the centre of a room in order to play it. The players take partners and line up facing each other in two equal rows. As everyone starts singing the song, 'The Grand Old Duke of York', the pair at the top of the line join hands and skip with a running side-step down the middle of the rows and back again. When they return to their places at the top of the line, they split and march down behind their lines to the other end. When they reach it, they face each other and continue singing, while the pair that are now at the top of the line join hands and skip down the middle as before. The game is completed when each pair has had a turn.

For those unfamiliar with the song, here are the words:

> *Oh, the Grand Old Duke of York,*
> *He had ten thousand men,*
> *He marched them up to the top of the hill,*
> *And he marched them down again.*
> *And when they were up, they were up,*
> *And when they were down, they were down,*
> *And when they were only half-way up,*
> *They were neither up nor down!*

MUSICAL HATS △

Players: *four or more*
Equipment: *hats for all but one player; a source of music*

The players sit in a circle, and all but one are given hats. These can be party paper hats or real hats, depending what is available. When the music starts, the players pass the hats round the circle. When it stops, all those with hats in their hands put them on their heads. The player left without a hat leaves the circle, and takes one hat with him or her. The game continues until only one player is left, and he or she wins.

AVOID-THE-HASSOCK DANCE △ △

Players: *four or more*
Equipment: *a hassock, or cushion, plus a source of music*

The hassock is placed on its end in the middle of the room, and the players form a small circle round it. A cushion can be stood on its end if no hassock is available. When the music starts, the players link arms and dance round the hassock. The aim of the game is that every player should try to pull every other player over the hassock, while everyone tries to prevent this happening to them. The players will be leaping around and moving backwards and forwards in their attempts to avoid the hassock. Anyone who knocks it over has to leave the game. The last player dancing round the standing hassock wins the game.

MUSICAL ISLANDS △ △

Players: *ten or more*
Equipment: *a number of 'islands' made of newspaper; a source of music*

A number of 'islands' are cut out of newspaper and scattered around the floor. The players glide gracefully around to the music and, when it stops, leap on to the nearest paper island. Anyone who fails to fit his or her feet on an island drops out, taking away one island. (A bit of common sense must be applied here. If there are ten islands and eight people drop out, eight islands shouldn't be removed all at once, or the game will be over much too quickly.) The last player left playing wins. Any player caught hovering near an island, when he or she is supposed to be gliding round the dance floor, may be disqualified.

O'GRADY SINGS △

Players; *any number*
Equipment: *none*

This game is a musical version of the famous Victorian parlour game 'O'Grady Says', set to music. The host stands in front of the guests, and gives them instructions. When he touches his toes and chants 'O'Grady sings do *this*', the players must follow suit. When he puts his hands on his head and chants, 'O'Grady sings do *this*', the players must follow suit. But when he scratches his nose and chants 'O'Grady sings do *that*', the players must *not* copy him. So whenever he sings 'Do this' they must copy, but whenever he sings 'Do that' they must not, or they will be eliminated from the game. The more rapidly the host (or hostess) can incant the orders the more confused the players will become, and the more fun everyone will have.

THE CONDUCTOR △ ♀

Players: *any number*
Equipment: *none*

If you have ever seen yourself as leader of the London Symphony Orchestra, this is the game for you. It is not one for shrinking violets, or anyone who doesn't mind appearing foolish, so tends to be enjoyed most when players have had a few glasses of wine. The conductor stands facing the other players, and gives each of them an imaginary instrument. When the conductor begins to clap, each player must begin to play his or her instrument making the right kind of noises to match. When the conductor stops clapping, and begins to imitate the movements of one of the players, by drawing the bow across a violin, beating a drum, or blowing a trumpet, all the other players, except the one being imitated, must stop playing, so that one player and the conductor are left performing a duet. The conductor can change instruments as often as he or she pleases, and any players who carry on playing their instruments after the conductor has changed to another one, or any player who fails to notice that the conductor has changed to his or her particular instrument, drops out. The game is best played fast and furiously, with the conductor changing instruments as often as possible, and bringing in the whole orchestra from time to time by clapping his or her hands.

PASS THE PARCEL MARK I △ △

Players: *any number*
Equipment: *an object to be wrapped, lots of wrapping paper, and a source of music*

The better prepared the object, the more fun everyone will have. A small object – say an apple, a pocket dictionary, or a small box of chocolates – is wrapped in a great many layers of paper to make a large parcel. The players form a circle and pass the parcel clockwise round the group while the music plays. Whoever is holding it at the time the music stops drops out of the game, and the last person in is allowed to unwrap the parcel and keep the prize.

PASS THE PARCEL MARK II △ △

Players: *any number*
Equipment: *as above*

Again, the players form a circle and pass the parcel clockwise round the group, but this time whoever is holding it when the music stops is allowed to remove one layer of the parcel's wrapping. The person who removes the last layer (and the parcel has to keep moving while the music is playing), keeps the prize.

MUSICAL NUMBERS △

Players: *any number*
Equipment: *a source of music*

As the music plays, the guests dance around the room in time to it. The moment it stops, the host or hostess calls out a number. It might be 'Twos', 'Threes', 'Fives', 'Eights', or whatever they fancy, and the players have to rush into groups of the given number. Any player who fails to join such a group is out, and the last one, or last pair, left in, win.

MUSICAL RUSH △

Players: *any number*
Equipment: *a number of small objects, plus a source of music*

A number of small objects are placed on the floor in the middle of the room – pencils, buttons, badges, coins, corks or whatever – and the players dance in time to the music round the objects, but at least two metres away from them. When the music stops, the players must rush forward and pick up an object, holding it out on the palm of the hand for everyone to see. As there are fewer objects than players, one will be unsuccessful, and he or she must drop out, taking one object away too. The rest are replaced, and the last player left dancing wins.

ZOUNDS SOUNDS ✍

Players: *any number*
Equipment: *a tape or cassette recorder; pencil and paper for each player*

This game needs preparing well in advance, but is well worth taking time and trouble over. The host or hostess must record a varied selection of snatches of sound, none lasting longer than ten seconds, which are played to the guests, who have to note down the identity of the sounds. The player with the highest number of correct answers wins. A brief 'miaow', a moment of Madonna, a bit of the Beatles, a snippet of Sibelius, the striking of a match, a dripping tap, a snatch of *Madame Butterfly*, the chirrup of a sparrow, the hostess's laugh, would all add up to an absorbing two minutes of novelty and noise.

Naughty Games

Ankles
Scrum
Morning Rush
Ghosts
Impossible Situations
Spend a Penny
Body Painting
Feeding Time
Postman's Knock
Feelies
Great Lovers
Mole Meetings
Kiss, Piggy, Kiss
Naughty Word Crossword
Sexy Numbers
Slave Market
Asset Stripping
Transvestite Dressing-up Race
Shopping List

ANKLES △

Players: *any number*
Equipment: *a screen, or blankets or sheets; pencil and paper for
each player*

Sauciness is in the eye of the beholder. The best Naughty Games
are those which *feel* naughty at the time of playing, but which
don't cause embarrassment when remembered in the cold light of
dawn. They give minxish pleasure, but no real cause for regret.
Ankles is just such a game – for saints who want to play at being
sinners without tarnishing their haloes. The players divide into
two teams, one team being sent from the room while the other
take off their shoes, socks and tights, and stand or sit behind a
large screen, so that from the far side only their feet and ankles
can be seen. If a screen is not available, the players may lie side
by side on the floor covered from head to shin in a blanket or
sheet. The other team then enters the room and starts to
examine the various feet and ankles. They may handle them if
necessary, but tickling, in the hope of eliciting an identifiable
giggle, is strictly forbidden. The inspecting team makes a list of
the names to which they think the feet belong, and the person in
the team who identifies the greatest number of feet and ankles
wins. The teams then reverse roles.

This is a wonderful game for a large gathering, when forty or
so feet are displayed, particularly if the guests have been
forewarned, and the men come with toes camouflaged with nail
varnish and the hairs carefully shaved off.

SCRUM △ △ ☠ ♟

Players: *any number over ten*
Equipment: *a tape or chalk line down the centre of the room*

This game is simply an excuse for the players to enjoy some
healthy grope therapy. They form two teams and confront each
other, heads down, in rugby scrum formation across a line down
the centre of the room. The aim of each team is to cross the line

and to prevent the other team from doing so, so they indulge in a battle of strength in an attempt to move forward. The team that succeeds in doing so wins. The less the players wear the naughtier the game (and the more therapeutic the scrummage).

MORNING RUSH △

Players: *any even number*
Equipment: *jackets, ties, hats and newspapers for the men; slippers and housecoats for the women*

Don't be put off by the chauvinistic sound to this game – it is, but it's great fun as a race. The men stand at one end of the room with their jackets over their arms, their shirts undone and flapping in the breeze, and their ties untied. The women stand at the opposite end, preferably wearing housecoats over their party frocks, and slippers instead of their best shoes, with a bowler hat and newspaper at their feet. On the word 'Go!' the women rush over to their partners, do up their shirts, tie their ties, help them on with their jackets, for which they are rewarded with a kiss on the forehead from their partners. They then rush back to pick up the newspapers and bowler hats, which they place under their partner's arms and on their heads respectively. They then race for the door, where she kisses him goodbye and pushes him out of the room. The first player to get this far, having completed all the stages properly, wins.

For those who find the game too chauvinistic, suggest a different version. In this, the women have to have the finishing touches put to their hair, have to be helped into their jackets, handed a briefcase, a handbag and a newspaper and kissed on the cheek before being ushered out of the room by rumpled, pyjama-clad spouses.

GHOSTS △ 💀 ♉

Players: *any even number*
Equipment: *a white sheet for each woman guest*

This game, which has nothing to do with Ibsen or M. R. James, is perfect for Hallowe'en parties, engagement parties, and other eerie occasions. It is also the ideal game to play if the host cannot decide who should partner whom into dinner.

The men leave the room and while they are absent the women seat themselves on chairs, lie on the floor, or drape themselves over the piano, each completely covered with a white sheet. (Ghosts dressed in Liberty prints and pretty pastel colours tend to lose some of their spooky impact.) When the men return, each must pick a ghost and identify her. He may ask the ghost to shriek or moan, coo or cackle; he may feel it all over (but only through the sheet), and he may ask it to perform little tasks. At no time may the ghost actually speak, or remove her shroud. When a man guesses the identity of the ghost she emerges from beneath the sheet and becomes his partner. If he fails to identify the ghost he first encounters, he can swap ghosts with another equally unsuccessful individual. Once all the ghosts have been unmasked, dinner is served.

IMPOSSIBLE SITUATIONS 🗫 💀 ♉

Players: *any number*
Equipment: *a number of prepared story endings, written on pieces of paper*

Many people enjoy telling slightly risqué stories but are held back by a natural and not unbecoming English reticence. This game liberates the saucy storyteller by giving him or her an acceptable framework within which to weave the tale. Each player is required to make up a story, the climax of which must be the 'impossible situation' handed to him or her by the host or hostess two minutes before the story was due to be told. The 'impossible situations' have, of course, to be prepared in advance.

One player might get a sentence like this: 'So there I was, in the middle of Piccadilly, with my trousers round my ankles, Julian's rhino whip in my hand, and an eight-foot-tall policeman approaching rapidly from a westerly direction.' Another might get, 'And it wasn't until we'd finished dinner that I discovered I was meant to do a belly dance in front of the Sultan.' Equipped with these last lines, the players would have to tell a story which led logically up to them. When everyone has had a go, the players vote for the most plausibly ingenious story. The game can be given a literary refinement by requiring the players to recount their stories in the manner of a particular author. Thus one might have to fit his or her story into the style of Margaret Drabble, or D. H. Lawrence, or Thomas Hardy.

SPEND A PENNY △ 💀 💀

Players: *one at a time*
Equipment: *a tenpenny piece in a bucket of water, plus lots of pennies*

Before the party, the host or hostess places a tenpenny piece at the bottom of a bucket of water. During the course of the evening, when any guest approaches nervously, asking for the 'little girls' room', or some other euphemism, the host or hostess leads them to the bucket (which might induce a momentary panic) and gives them a penny, telling them that they will only be shown the whereabouts of the loo when they have successfully dropped the penny on top of the tenpence.

BODY PAINTING △ 💀 🍷

Players: *any number*
Equipment: *body paints, brushes, newspapers to cover the carpet*

This game is a form of creative therapy used extensively in psychiatric hospitals throughout the Western world. It has even been practised in Montessori nursery schools. The players divide into groups of two or three and take off their clothes (or *some* of their clothes, if they're shy), for this *is* a naughty game. Each group is provided with an assortment of body paints, which are available from any good supplier of artists' materials, and invited to paint one another. The artists must paint together, so Adam will be daubing Brenda's knees while Brenda is dabbing Clara's arm and Clara is colouring Adam's apple.

No one should contemplate this game unless they have adequate central heating, enough newspapers to cover the carpets, and a shower with which to wash down the guests before they depart. A prize can be offered for the most beautifully painted body. Parties to which in-laws and maiden aunts have been invited are *not* the kind at which this game should be played.

FEEDING TIME △ ♀

Players: *any even number*
Equipment: *bibs and babies' bottles*

The women players sit on chairs at one end of the room, holding bibs and half-filled babies' bottles, complete with teats, while the men stand opposite their partners at the other end of the room. When the signal is given, the men rush over to their partners and sit on their laps. The women put the bibs round the men's necks and proceed to feed them as quickly as they can. The men may cling to the women, but may not touch the bottles with their hands. As soon as the bottle is emptied, the woman unties the bib and she and her 'baby' race back to the line from which the men started. The first pair over the finishing line are the winners, and the roles are then reversed, with the men feeding the women.

The bottles can be filled with anything from milk to champagne – though half a bottle of whisky might be a bit much. If you don't want the guests to get too drunk, then wine mixed with mineral water is a good bet. Or you might like to try a liquid aphrodisiac, such as almond soup (there's no guarantee that it works). Galen, second-century-AD court physician to Emperor

Marcus Aurelius, recommended a honey drink, mixed with crushed almonds and tiny grains of pine tree. But an egg flip would probably do just as well, since *The Perfumed Garden* says that 'he who eats the yolk of three eggs every day' (this, of course, was pre-Edwina Currie) will be sexually invigorated. The *Kama Sutra* favours a mixture of milk hedge plant and kantaka plant, mixed with monkey droppings and the powdered root of the lanjalika plant. Fortunately, you were not supposed to eat it, but to throw it at the woman of your choice. On reflection, it's probably safer to stick to milk.

POSTMAN'S KNOCK △ △ ♀

Players: *any number*
Equipment: *none*

This innocent and ancient pastime probably predates the first postman, who appeared on the scene in 1529. A male player leaves the room while those inside give themselves numbers – even numbers for the men, and uneven numbers for the women. When they have agreed their numbers, they call out, 'We're ready!' whereupon the 'postman' outside knocks firmly on the door three times, 'Who's there?' cry out the players in the room. ''Tis I, the postman,' replies the man outside, 'and I have something here for Number Three (or Five, or Seven, or any uneven number). Come and get it!' So Number Three goes out to join the postman, who gives her a kiss. The pair then return to the room and another player – female this time – leaves the room and becomes the postmistress. The remaining players choose new numbers, and the postmistress knocks and declares she has something for Number Four, or any other even number, and the player goes out to receive his kiss. If the postman or postmistress get his or her odd or even numbers mixed up and has to kiss someone of the same sex, then that's their problem (or their choice!)

FEELIES △ ♀

Players: *any number*
Equipment: *feather dusters; a source of music*

This jolly game needs a warm house in which to play it, for it requires the players to dance around, scantily clad, until the music stops, when they must 'freeze' on the spot. The host or hostess then wanders amongst them, armed with a feather duster, with which he or she tries to tickle their fancy and make them twitch or giggle. Anyone moving a muscle drops out, and has to join the host or hostess in the attempt to make the other players move. The music should be stopped and started frequently, and the ticklers should not be allowed more than ten seconds or so in which to do their dirty work. The last surviving 'statue' wins.

GREAT LOVERS 🖅 ☠ ♀

Players: *any even number*
Equipment: *none*

Two players leave the room. The remainder choose identities for them – real or imaginary – then invite them back in the room and tell them separately, and in whispers, whom they are to be. So, for example, Adam might be told that he must be Rudolf Valentino, and Eve might be Mary Whitehouse. And with their new-found personalities, neither of which is revealed to the other, they have to woo each other for five minutes. At the end of this time, Adam must guess Eve's identity, and vice versa.

For those who have ever wondered what the Queen Mother might do faced with a passionate Boy George, or Woody Allen faced with a smitten Patricia Routledge, this game provides as accurate an answer as they are ever likely to get. If the players are talented, a highly entertaining time will be had by all.

MOLE MEETINGS △ △ ☠ ☠ ♉

Players: *any number*
Equipment: *old blankets*

This is a highly risqué game, and the guests intended to play it must be chosen with care. The host or hostess constructs a 'tunnel' from the hallway to the living-room, or between two rooms of the house, from the old blankets. The guests have to undress, and then, naked or near naked, they must crawl through the tunnel toward the living-room, and on the journey meet and 'discover' other travelling moles. If they don't emerge from the tunnel after a few minutes, the host should threaten to remove the blankets!

KISS, PIGGY, KISS △ ♉

Players: *any number*
Equipment: *a blindfold*

The players form a circle, putting one of their number in the middle and blindfolding him or her. For one minute, they have to hop around in a circle holding hands, while the blindfolded figure in the centre revolves on his or her own axis in the reverse direction. When the hopping stops, the person in the middle walks to the edge of the circle and kisses the first person encountered. From the kiss, he or she must guess the identity of the person kissed. If the guess is correct, the player can take off the blindfold and pass it on to the person kissed, who must don it and take a turn in the middle. If, however, the blindfolded person cannot guess the identity of the person he or she kisses, or lights on a member of the same sex and doesn't fancy kissing, then he or she has to start all over again.

Keen Europeans will want to play a version of the game in which the central character gives a Swiss kiss to the person they bump into. Never heard of a Swiss kiss? It is, of course, simply a French kiss through which you yodel.

NAUGHTY WORD CROSSWORD 🗞🏴‍☠️🍷

Players: *two to six, or groups of that number*
Equipment: *pencils and squared paper, a die and shaker for
each group*

This game is a pencil and paper version of Scrabble, in which
players have to construct words which fit together in a grid. But
the catch is that all the words used have to be in some way
naughty.

Players shake the die for the highest score to start, and the one
who wins can construct the first word, with the number of letters
indicated by the score of the die. Thus, if the player throws a six,
he or she starts by writing down a six-letter word. The next
player throws the die, and has to construct a word which fits in
with the letters used in the first word and has the same number
of letters as the throw of the die. Thus play continues. Anyone
who cannot think of a naughty word or the right number of
letters which fits in the grid drops out of the game. Players score
one point for each letter of each
word they make, and the player
with the highest score wins. The
really hilarious part of the game
is trying to find a word which
everyone considers naughty
which fits into the grid. For
example, in this grid, the players would have to decide
whether LIMB is considered
naughty or not!

```
        F
        A       L
        R       I
   B O T T O M
   O       A B
   G   B R A
           T
```

SEXY NUMBERS 🔺🍷

Players: *any numbers*
Equipment: *none*

The host or hostess organizes the other guests into a circle, and
whispers to each of them a secret number. The men get even

numbers, the women uneven numbers. One player then stands in the middle of the circle. If the player is a man, he calls out two uneven numbers; if she is a woman, she calls out two even numbers. Then the numbered people rush forwards, and the first one to kiss the player in the middle takes his or her place, and has to call out numbers in turn. With a large party, this is an admirable getting-to-know-you and getting-to-know-if-I-like-the-taste-of-you game.

SLAVE MARKET △☠♀

Players: *eight or more*
Equipment: *counters, or coins, for bidding*

In male chauvinist households, the women are herded into a corner and put up for auction; in feminist households the men are herded into a corner and put up for auction. Whichever way round it is, the bidders are given counters or coins to allow them to bid, while the host acts as auctioneer. He tries to get as good a price as possible, while the players egg one another on and try to retain as many of their counters as they can while still securing the best buys. At the end of the auction, the bidder who has the greatest number of slaves wins. If two bidders have an equal number of slaves, then the one with the greatest number of counters or coins wins.

ASSET STRIPPING ✉ ☠

Players: *any number*
Equipment: *a tray covered with small objects, a cloth, and a pencil and paper for each player*

This is a naughty version of Kim's Game, in which, if you remember, twenty or thirty different objects are placed on a tray, the players are allowed to look at it for thirty seconds, and then the tray is covered up and the players have to list all the things that were on the tray. As this is a naughty version, you could put some of these things on the tray: a torn-out page-three-girl picture, a suspender, a jock strap, a copy of *Lady Chatterley's Lover*, a revealing piece of underwear, and so on, interspersed with a number of forgettable items, such as a pencil sharpener, an eraser, a thimble, a piece of chalk, a hair grip, a feather, etc. Now, in this version of the game, all those who list an item *not* on the tray, or all those who forget one or more items, have to remove a piece of their clothing. Obviously the better your memory, the more clothed you are at the end! The person who ends up with the most clothes on wins.

TRANSVESTITE DRESSING-UP RACE △ 🍷

Players: *two or more*
Equipment: *clothes to dress up in*

With a large number of guests (or a small number of available clothes) this race would have to be run in heats, but otherwise players simply race one against each other. The players line up at one end of the room, and opposite them, at the other end, are placed small piles of clothes – women's clothes opposite the men, and men's clothes opposite the women. If possible these clothes should include shoes, for it is extremely comical to watch men trying to hobble along in high-heeled shoes, and women flapping about in great big brogues! The piles should be as equal as possible, so each player has to put on the same number of items of clothing.

On the word 'Go!' the players dash across the room to their piles of clothing and put on one item. Once this is done they have to rush back to the starting line, and touch the wall, a chair, or whatever, and then dash back to the clothes again to put on another item. This continues until all the clothing has been put on (wise players will leave the shoes until last) and the players are back at the starting line. The first person back, suitably dressed, wins the race.

SHOPPING LIST △ ☠

Players: *any large number*
Equipment: *pencil and paper*

One player is the shopper, and the others, in teams of four to six, represent rival department stores. The shopper makes up a list of items which some, at least, of the players might be expected to have about their person, and the game can be made as naughty, or as innocent, as the guests indicate. So, for example, the shopper might ask the stores to supply him or her with: a pair of tights, a photograph of a naked lady or a piece of knicker elastic, or simply ask for things like a key ring holding five keys, a bus ticket, a 19p stamp, and so on. A point is awarded to the first 'store' to supply the shopper with the item, and the store with the most points at the end of the game wins.

Allsorts

Put and Take
Lotto
Chicago
Going to Boston
Craps
Fours
Ends
Maltese Cross
Tiddlywinks
Calculator Pontoon

PUT AND TAKE △

Players: *any number*
Equipment: *a Put and Take top (see illustration)*

The top can be made by cutting out an eight-sided figure from stiff card and marking it as shown, PUT 1 is opposite PUT 4; TAKE 1 opposite TAKE 4; PUT 3 opposite PUT ALL; and TAKE 3 opposite TAKE ALL. A nail is then pushed through the centre of the top so that it can be spun and land on one edge.

Each player puts an agreed stake into the pot. Then each player in turn spins the top, and according to the face that is uppermost when it comes to rest, puts the indicted amount into the pot or takes the indicated amount out of the pot. PUT ALL means that the player must put into the pot a sum equal to the amount already there; TAKE ALL means that he or she wins the entire pot. The winner is the player who ends up with the most money, or counters, or who is instructed to TAKE ALL.

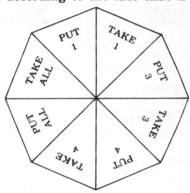

LOTTO △

Players: *two to six*
Equipment: *Lotto cards; ninety numbered discs*

Lotto, also known as Housey Housey or Tombola, is the forerunner of the modern, commercialized Bingo. Each player has a special card marked with fifteen numbers between 1 and 90, and none of the numbers is duplicated on other cards.

One of the players is the caller. He or she has a set of ninety numbered discs which are drawn at random, one at a time, from a bag or box. As each number is drawn, the caller calls it out, and the disc bearing the number is given to the player on whose card it appears. That player covers the number on his or her card with the disc. When all the numbers on a player's card have been covered he or she calls out 'Lotto!' and wins the game.

	12		31		53		72	84
4		24		46	65			87
	19	28		49		68	77	

CHICAGO △△

Players: *two or more*
Equipment: *two dice*

This is a simple game of luck based on the eleven possible totals which can be obtained from throwing two dice, i.e. totals from 2 to 12. The dice pass round the table eleven times, each player in turn throwing the two dice once. On the first round, each player who throws the dice to make a total of 2 scores two points; the others score nothing. On the second round, each player who throws the dice to make a total of 3 scores three points, the others scoring nothing. Thus the game proceeds, with the players having to score totals of 4, 5, 6 and so on up to 12 on successive rounds, and scoring accordingly. The player with the highest total score wins.

GOING TO BOSTON △

Players: *two or more*
Equipment: *three dice*

The first player in this game rolls all three dice at once. Leaving the die which shows the highest number, or, if two are equally high, leaving only one of them, he or she rolls the other two again. Of these two, the player again leaves the die showing the higher number and rolls the other die again. This completes his or her turn, and the score is the total shown by the three dice. When all the players have followed this routine in turn, the player with the highest score wins the round. The game is played for an agreed number of rounds, and the player who wins the most rounds is the overall winner of the game.

CRAPS

Players: *two or more*
Equipment: *two dice; a supply of counters, buttons, etc., for use as stakes*

Craps is a gambling game, which is often played for high stakes. It can, however, be played in a friendly fashion for pennies, counters or buttons. Each player takes a turn to be the 'shooter', or person who throws the dice, and he or she puts on the table whatever stake he or she is prepared to wager. All or part of this stake may be matched or 'covered' by the other players.

The shooter throws the two dice. If the total value is 7 or 11 this is known as a 'natural', and the shooter immediately wins all the stakes that have been wagered. If the total of the two dice is 2, 3 or 12 this is known as the 'craps', and the shooter immediately loses. If the shooter throws any other total on his or her first throw, i.e. 4, 5, 6, 8, 9 or 10, this is known as his or her 'point'. He or she then continues throwing until either the point is thrown again or until a 7 is thrown (any other total thrown being disregarded). If the point comes up first, then the shooter wins; if a 7 comes up first then the shooter loses.

As long as the shooter wins, he or she retains the dice, places a new stake and shoots again. But as soon as he or she loses, the dice are passed to the next player, who then becomes the shooter.

FOURS △

Players: *three, four or five*
Equipment: *a set of dominoes*

In this simple domino game the lead player is chosen by lot, and each player then draws his or her dominoes. If three are playing, each draws nine dominoes; if four are playing, each draws seven dominoes; if five, each draws five dominoes. Any dominoes left over are put to one side and are not used in the game.

The object of the game is to be the first player to get rid of all the dominoes. Each player in turn can continue playing dominoes for as long as he or she can match either end of the line of dominoes already played, after which the turn passes to the next player on the left.

The first player leads with any domino he or she cares to play from the hand he or she holds, and continues playing until he or she can no longer go. If very lucky, he or she will be able to play all the dominoes in one turn, and if so, will win the game. However, it usually takes at least two turns to get rid of the dominoes, and each player plays in turn until one player wins the game by getting rid of all their dominoes. If the game becomes blocked and no one can go, each player adds up the number of pips on the dominoes left in his or her hand, and the player with the lowest total wins.

ENDS △

Players: *four*
Equipment: *set of dominoes*

Each player draws seven dominoes, and the game begins by the player with the double 6 placing it face upwards in the centre of the table. Each player in turn is then allowed to play one domino that matches either end of the line of dominoes already played, the turn passing to the next player on the left round the table. If a player cannot go when it is his or her turn, he or she must ask the player on the left for a suitable domino. If that player has such a domino, then it must be given to the person who has asked for it, who then plays it. The player on the left then has his or her turn as usual. If the player on the left does not have a playable domino, he or she must ask the player on *his or her* left, and so on until a player in the chain is found who *does* have a playable domino, who must give it to the player who first requested it, and play proceeds as normal. If the request passes right round the table and no player has a playable domino, then the player who first asked for it is allowed to play *any* domino from his or her hand on either end of the line, without making a match. The player who gets rid of all his or her dominoes first, wins.

MALTESE CROSS ✎

Players: *four*
Equipment: *a set of dominoes*

Each of the four players draws seven dominoes, and the player with the double 6 starts. Dominoes may be played to both ends and both sides of the double 6 so a four-ended line of play results. However, in this game, until a double has been played, play is blocked. Look at the example illustrated overleaf. The player whose turn it is to go may play any matching domino at a) or c), since the double 6 and double 4 have been played. But only the double 1 may be played at b), and the double 3 at d). Players unable to play a domino when it is their turn must pass. The first player to get rid of all his or her dominoes wins. If the game becomes blocked, then the winner is the player with the lowest number of pips left.

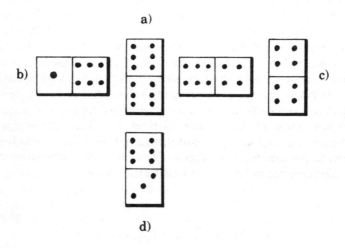

a)

b)

c)

d)

TIDDLYWINKS

Players: *two, three or four*
Equipment: *cup; six winks and a squidger for each player*

Twiddlywinks is best played on a table covered with a thick cloth or piece of felt. The cup, which should be about an inch or two high and about an inch and a half wide, is placed in the centre of the table. Each players is given six 'winks' – small, flat discs, and a 'squidger', which is a larger disc. (Each player has winks and squidger of one colour, usually red, blue, green or yellow.) The object of the game is to squidge all one's winks into the cup, and this is achieved by pressing the edge of the squidger against the wink, thus making it jump into the air and, hopefully, land in the cup.

Each player lines up his or her winks at an equal distance from the cup. The order of play is determined by each player squidging one wink, and the player who gets nearest to the cup starts. Play proceeds from person to person in a clockwise direction. Players can only squidge their own winks, and have one squidge per turn, except when they have potted a wink, when they may have an extra squidge. Like golf balls, winks must always be squidged from where they lie, except when they fall off the table, in which case they may be placed on the edge of the table and squidged from there. If a wink becomes covered by another wink, it is said to be 'squopped', and when this happens a player may not remove the opponent's wink nor squidge it; he or she must wait until the opponent removes it, or attempt to dislodge it by squidging another wink of his or her own at it. Thus successful play requires not only accurate squidging, but also the ability to judge when to pot and when to squop. The first player who successfully squidges all his or her winks into the cup wins.

CALCULATOR PONTOON

Players: *any small number*
Equipment: *two dice; a pocket calculator per player*

Here's a game for the 1990s, in which every person is expected to have a personal computer, or at least a pocket calculator. In the game, each player in turn rolls the two dice. One determines the number to be entered on the calculator; the other, the arithmetic operation to be entered, an odd number indicating subtraction, and an even number addition. The player may choose which of the dice to use as a number, and which to use as an operation. For example, a throw of 4, 3 may be entered on the calculator as 4– or 3+. The aim of the game is to reach a displayed total of exactly 21, and the first player to do so is the winner.

For example:

Dice rolled	Number entered	Number display
6, 2	6 +	6
3, 2	3 +	9
4, 4	4 +	13
4, 3	3 +	16
6, 1	1 +	17
6, 3	3 +	20
4, 5	4 −	16
4, 5	5 +	21

Highbrow Games

Frances Hodgson Burnett's Game
ABC
Style
Bluffo
Stinkety Pinkety
No, No, Nijinsky!
The Rupert Murdoch Game
Politix
Rules
When in Rome
Quotations Mark I
Quotations Mark II
Tennis Coude Fuss
What is the Question to this Answer?

FRANCES HODGSON BURNETT'S GAME 📜

Players: *two to ten*
Equipment: *none*

This game was said to be a favourite of the popular author of *The Secret Garden* and *Little Lord Fauntleroy*. It involves one player standing up and telling the rest what he or she likes and does not like. When one of the players thinks he or she understands the rationale of why this is, he or she raises a hand and gives an example of what he or she thinks the former player likes and does not like. He or she should not explain how the player chooses his or her likes and dislikes. If the second player is right, they are congratulated, and another player has a go. The last player to give an example loses, and has to pay a forfeit (or wash up).

Here is an example. Can you spot what the likes and dislikes are?

I like coffee, but I don't like tea.

I like cabbage, but I don't like cauliflower.

I like green, but I don't like red.

I like boots but I don't like shoes.

I like butterflies, but I don't like moths.

I like bees, but I don't like wasps.

I like football, but I don't like golf.

I like tennis, but I don't like cricket.

I like *Little Lord Fauntleroy*, but I don't like *The Secret Garden*.

All the things I like have a pair of vowels or consonants side by side, but the things I don't like do not include such a pair.

ABC 🔺

Players: *any number*
Equipment: *none*

The organizer of this game must judge the level of his or her guests' brows very carefully. If it is made too easy, they will find it dull; if it is made too difficult, the guests will feel inadequate and uncomfortable. He or she must prepare a series of demanding questions about any subject under the sun: for instance, name a newspaper proprietor, a poet who wrote exclusively in alexandrines, a boxer, a member of the Bloomsbury set, a nineteenth-century philosopher, a mineral, or whatever. Having read out the questions, the host or hostess announces a letter of the alphabet – either plucked from the air or chosen by sticking a pin into a newspaper – and the first player to name a newspaper proprietor or a nineteenth-century philosopher beginning with that letter gains a point. The player who gains the greatest number of points wins.

STYLE

Players: *any number*
Equipment: *pencils and paper*

This game is one for literate and literary types. The players are supplied with pencils and pieces of paper, and they write down on it the name of a writer, or of a newspaper, magazine, or advertising agency. The papers are then collected, shuffled and redistributed, and the players then have to write a short paragraph on a given theme – Modern Morals, the Channel Tunnel, the Nude in Photography – and so on, in the style of the writer, newspaper, magazine or advertising agency prescribed on the paper they have just been given. A few sentences on the theme of 'sex in old-age pensioners' in the style of Charles Dickens, Catherine Cookson, *Time Out, The Sun*, and Saatchi and Saatchi, would provide both fun and a challenge in almost any writers' circle.

BLUFFO 🎓

Players: *any even number up to twelve*
Equipment: *paper and pencil*

This game is loosely based on the popular television panel game hosted by Robert Robinson, *Call My Bluff*. As in the television programme, the players are divided into two teams, who go into separate corners to decide who is going to do what. The host or hostess provides each team with a series of categories, depending on the players' particular interests, such as Plays, Animals, Scientific Discoveries, and so on. If Team A has four members and the first category is Plays, then each member of Team A will have to tell the members of Team B about a particular play. Three of the plays thus described will be entirely imaginary, but one will be a real play, and Team B must work out which one it is. If they do so, they gain a point. If they pick one of the bluffs, Team A gains a point. The teams take it in turns to present their true and false information, and the team that is the more successful in spotting the truth in their opponents, and concealing it from them themselves, will gain the most points and win.

STINKETY PINKETY 🎓 🎓

Players: *any number*
Equipment: *none*

Players divide into pairs or small groups, and one person offers a definition. The other player(s) must then translate the definition into a noun modified by a rhyming adjective. So, for example, 'an overweight piece of headgear' would be 'a fat hat'; 'a particularly stupid donkey' would be 'a crass ass'. These simple examples, in which both nouns and adjectives are monosyllabic, are called Stink Pinks.

One stage more difficult are Stinky Pinkies, which call for nouns and adjectives of two syllables which both rhyme. Thus 'a foolish fellow called William' would be 'a Silly Billy'; 'the uppermost storey of a house that won't move even in an earthquake' would be 'a static attic'.

Stinkety Pinkety is the third stage of the game, which requires trisyllabic nouns and adjectives with the last two syllables rhyming. Thus 'a dull work of art produced by joining together minute pieces of glass and stone' would be 'a prosaic mosaic'; 'a southern German baby delivered by means of surgery' would be 'a Bavarian Caesarian'. The first player to offer a suitable Stink Pink, Stinky Pinky or Stinkety Pinkety gains a point, and becomes the person offering the definitions in the next round. The player with the greatest number of points wins.

NO, NO, NIJINSKY! ✑

Players: *any number*
Equipment: *none*

This is a game for specialists, which should only be played at parties where the majority of the guests have something in common. Since the aim of the game is for one player to get up and give a detailed impersonation of a well-known figure in a particular field, a ballet dancer performing a well-observed caricature of Nijinsky doing a series of complex double *entrechats* would be wasting his talents on an audience of computer programmers and chartered accountants. The brilliance of the dancer's performance and the accuracy of his impersonation could only be properly appreciated by other ballet buffs. Actors, secretaries, civil servants, electrical engineers and architects, imitating other actors, secretaries, civil servants, electrical engineers and architects, will vastly entertain actors, secretaries, civil servants, electrical engineers and architects, but probably no one else. No one really wins this game, though points can be awarded for the brilliance of the impersonation, and to the player(s) who guess the answer.

THE RUPERT MURDOCH GAME 🖎

Players: *six or more*
Equipment: *none*

Rupert Murdoch, otherwise known as the 'dirty Digger', is the Australian-born tycoon who seems to have managed to gain control of a sizeable chunk of the media in Great Britain without being referred to the Monopolies Commission. *The Times, The Sunday Times, The Sun*, Collins the publishers, Sky Television – all are his. The aim of this game is for the other players to persuade 'Rupert Murdoch' to invest his money in a business proposition which they outline to him. Each player has five minutes to present his or her scheme, and when he or she has heard all the proposals, 'Rupert Murdoch' has to indicate which one he will back, for how much, and why. The player who receives the most support from the businessman extraordinary, is the winner. His or her prize is a copy of the *Daily Mirror*.

POLITIX 🖎

Players: *any number*
Equipment: *none*

This is a game about politics, much loved by politicians, actual or aspiring, and political pundits, professional or amateur, and played regularly at Blackpool and Brighton at Party Conference time. The politically naive – i.e. most voters and members of the House of Lords – might find the game a bore, but those who regard themselves as 'politically aware' will adore it because it gives them a chance to show off. The players form a circle, and one says a word, a name or a phrase which has a specific political connotation. The player on his or her left (or right, depending on your politics) must follow with another word, name or phrase directly associated with the first word, name or phrase. The next player must do the same, and so on round the circle, until a player falters or says a word which is challenged and the challenge is upheld by the politically acute umpire. Thus the first player might start with Richard Livsey (SLD, Brecon and Radnor), whom he happens to know. The next player, more politically astute, and having done his or her homework, could say Alan Meale (Lab., Mansfield) who had an equal lowest majority in the 1987 election with Mr Livsey of 56 votes. Thinking of low majorities, the third player could offer Gerald Bowden (Con., Dulwich) who had the lowest Conservative majority of 180. The fourth player might feel a bit stumped, but if blessed with a long memory could say Sam Silkin (MP for Dulwich in 1979) – and so the game could go on. If your favourite reading is *Hansard*, this is the game for you. Any players who cannot think of legitimate political associations drop out, and the winner is the last one left in.

RULES 🎓

Players: *any number*
Equipment: *a book of 'rules'*

This, too, is a game for specialists, and it can only be played if all the players have at least one interest in common. It is a quiz game, in which the host or hostess is armed with a book of 'rules' from which to put questions to the guests, and the winner is the player who knows the rules best. At a party of prison officers the 'rules' might be the Home Office *Prison Rules*; at a get-together of young mothers the 'rules' might be Dr Spock's *Baby and Child Care*; at a gathering of Bahais the 'rules' might be *The Proclamation of Bahá'u'lláh*; at a gathering of learner drivers, or of driving instructors, they might be the *Highway Code*. Most professions and interest groups have some sort of 'rule book', which provides plenty of material for a testing quiz. The winner is the person who gets the greatest number of correct answers.

WHEN IN ROME 📜

Players: *any number*
Equipment: *pencil and paper*

What do these words have in common: LID, CIVIL, MILD, MIX? They
are all formed from letters that are also Roman numerals: C, D, I,
L, M, V, X. In this game, players are given five minutes in which to
list as many words as they can using only these letters. The
player with the longest list wins. The wearing of togas is
optional.

QUOTATIONS MARK I 📜

Players: *any number*
Equipment: *a dictionary of quotations*

Messing about in quotes is one of the most enjoyable of literary
pursuits. In this game, the host or hostess, equipped with a
dictionary of quotations, reads out a series of memorable phrases
and invites the other players to identify who said what and in
what context. One mark is awarded for the author and one for
the context, and the player with the most marks at the end of the
game wins. The more obvious the quotation, the less entertaining the game. Margaret Thatcher's remark, 'No woman in my
time will be Prime Minister,' will challenge no one, but her
comment on modern life, 'Most of us have stopped using silver
every day,' may well puzzle a number of players. In selecting
suitable *mots*, the host or hostess should aim to be judicious, not
obscure.

QUOTATIONS MARK II 🕮 🕮

Players: *any number*
Equipment: *a dictionary of quotations*

The players sit in a circle and quote quotes at each other, from memory. The second player must quote a quote which contains at least one word which was in the first player's quote; the third player's must contain at least one word which was in the second player's; and so on. If a player cannot think of an appropriate quotation, or invents one and is challenged by another player whose challenge is upheld by the dictionary of quotations, the guilty party drops out. The last player left quoting is the winner. With a well-read assortment of guests, it might go something like this: 'He is rich that is satisfied' (Thomas Fuller); 'It is easier for a camel to go through the eye of a needle, than for a rich man to enter the kingdom of God' (St Matthew); 'Man appoints, and God disappoints' (Cervantes); 'A man in the house is worth two in the street' (Mae West); 'Daughter I am in my mother's house, but mistress in my own' (Kipling) – and so on.

TENNIS COUDE FUSS 🕮 🕮

Players: *any number*
Equipment: *none*

This is an international version of the Tennis, Elbow, Foot Game, in which players form a circle and take it in turns to call out words, each word being either directly related to the previous word, or rhyming with it, such as: tennis, elbow, foot, shoe, loo, chain, reaction, and so on. In this version, the principle is the same, but the game must be played in several languages. Each word must have an association with, or must rhyme with, the previous word, but it should also be in a different language from the previous word. Players are disqualified if they use words that don't really link up or rhyme with the previous word, or if they are in the same language as it. Thus a game might begin like this: *'Teniso'* (Esperanto); *'Coude'* (French); *'Fuss'* (German);

'*Futbalo*' (Esperanto); '*Jeu*' (French); '*Mat*' (Russian); '*Hat*' (English); and so on. It's a game guaranteed to enliven even the deadliest diplomatic function.

WHAT IS THE QUESTION TO THIS ANSWER?

Players: *any number*
Equipment: *none*

This is a game for the obtuse, abstruse and immensely high-powered. The host or hostess must supply a series of erudite and/or meaningless 'answers', to which the players must find -appropriate questions. In each case, the question generally regarded as the most brilliant earns a mark. And the person who collects the most marks is a great thinker, or a clapped-out philosophy don, or both, which is unlikely. If the host or hostess says as his answer, 'What is the question to this answer?' the most brilliant player will be the one who offers 'What is the answer to this question?' Or vice versa. This *is* a highbrow game.

Quickies

Mouth Ball
Kerpow!
Monosyllabics
Nightcap
One-minute Walk
Thimble Race
Rhyme in Time
Rhyme Round
Knickers!
Breath Test
Number or Your Life
Tebahpla
Tissue Tournament
Tongue-twisters

MOUTH BALL △

Players: *eight or more*
Equipment: *a spoon for each player, and two ping-pong balls*

This amusing end-of-the-evening frolic will leave everyone feeling jolly, and can be played even as guests are donning their coats to depart. All the players are given a spoon each, which they must hold between their teeth and not touch with their hands. They can be divided into two teams and stand in two lines. The leader of each team is then given a ping-pong ball, which is placed on his or her spoon. If no ping-pong balls are available, then marbles, radishes or nuts would suffice. Eggs tend to be too heavy for anyone with false teeth. The leaders then pass the balls from their spoons to the spoons of the next in line, and so they are passed down the line, with the first team to get the ball to the last player without touching it with the hands, or dropping it, winning. If the ball is dropped, it must be picked up using only mouth and spoon – no hands.

KERPOW! △△

Players: *any number*
Equipment: *none*

The players form a circle and link their little fingers. (This has absolutely nothing to do with the game, but it is fun, and since fun is what it's all about, it's worth trying.) Fingers linked, the players start counting: 'One, two, three, four' until they reach five, or a multiple of five, when the player involved says 'Kerpow!' instead. When they reach seven or a multiple of seven, the player involved says 'Splat!' instead. Anyone who falters, fumbles, faints, says a multiple of five or seven, or who says 'Splat!' instead of 'Kerpow!', or vice versa, is out. The last player left counting wins.

MONOSYLLABICS △

Players: *any number*
Equipment: *none*

This game, originally popularized by the late Kenneth Tynan and George Melly, and much favoured by Lady Antonia Fraser, is more demanding than it sounds. The players must talk only in words of one syllable. Anyone who utters a word of more than one syllable drops out of the game. It is a good game to play when the party is getting out of hand, the neighbours starting to complain, and you are longing to go to bed. When people are reduced to words of one syllable, conversation can quickly come to a standstill!

NIGHTCAP △△

Players: *any number*
Equipment: *babies' feeding bottles, lengths of string, and beverages to put in the bottles*

This is not so much a game, more a way of providing an eccentric nightcap. As many babies' bottles as there are guests are filled with an assortment of beverages suitable for the particular guests – black coffee for the drivers, cocoa for the insomniacs, whisky for the boozers – and suspended, teats downwards, on pieces of string at just below head height. The player who empties his or her bottle first, wins.

ONE-MINUTE WALK △

Players: *any number*
Equipment: *a stop-watch*

This is a good game to play when everyone is about to leave the party, for it rounds off the evening entertainingly and only takes one minute. All the players have to do is to walk from one end of the room to the other in precisely one minute – no more, no less. Their watches are confiscated, the clocks in the room are veiled, and the players are told to walk steadily and at an even pace. Players who stop in mid-walk, or who arrive at the winning post before the minute is up, are out. The host or hostess holds the stop-watch, tells the players when to start, and cries 'Halt!' when the minute is up. The player nearest his or her destination at that time is the winner.

THIMBLE RACE △ △

Players: *eight or more*
Equipment: *a straw for each player; two thimbles*

Thimbles, like chastity and muffins, may be disappearing from modern life, but you must be able to find a couple with which to play this game. The players are divided into two teams, provided with a straw each, which they place in their mouths, and have to race to pass a thimble from the leader to the last person in line by balancing it on the end of their straws. No hands are allowed, and if a thimble is dropped, as it is being gingerly transferred from one straw to another, the player must pick it up by dextrous use of the straw only. The first team to end with the thimble balanced on the last player's straw, wins.

RHYME IN TIME 📖

Players: *any number*
Equipment: *none*

In this game, the players must converse in verse, and anyone who talks in anything else must pay a forfeit. The game tends to start slowly, but once players have got into the mood, rhyming conversation usually flows easily. If by any chance it doesn't, it is best to abandon the game.

RHYME ROUND ✑

Players: *any number*
Equipment: *none*

More simple amusement of a versified kind is provided by this game. The players sit in a circle and converse, each player beginning their remark with a word that rhymes with the last word spoken by a preceding player. For example, 'Is Harry Higgins wearing a *wig*?' asks Annie. '*Big* Bertie's propping up the *door*,' replies Brian. '*Cor*, isn't this party a *bore*?' asks Claire. '*Whore* Samantha's enjoying herself, the *cow*,' remarks Dave. '*Wow*, you're in a mood tonight, *ducky*,' chirrups Ed. '*Mucky* stuff, this wine, isn't *it*?' complains Fred, and so it goes on. Anyone faltering or missing a rhyme, drops out, and the last player left talking wins.

KNICKERS! △△

Players: *any number*
Equipment: *none*

For some reason the word 'knickers' in guaranteed to make people laugh whenever it is uttered. In this game, players bombard a victim with ridiculous questions, such as 'What is your favourite supper?' 'What do you dream about at night?' 'What did you give your fiancée for Christmas?' – to all of which the victim must reply, 'Knickers!', and do so in deadly earnest. If the victim laughs, chuckles, giggles, or even smiles, he or she is out. If he or she can withstand two minutes of persistent and impertinent questions, answering 'Knickers!' to every one without laughing, the victim wins.

BREATH TEST △ ∧ ♀

Players: *any number*
Equipment: *a mug of black coffee, a piece of cheese, and a balloon for each player*

One London host used to ask his guests to walk down a straight white line before they drove home at the end of the evening. If they seemed unsteady, they were sent home by taxi, and the host sent his chauffeur after them with their car. If you don't have a white line painted on your drawing-room floor, or a live-in chauffeur, this game is a good substitute. In a jolly sort of way, it has a very sobering effect on the players, and is a good, quick game with which to wind up a party. The players stand in a circle, each armed with a mug of black coffee, a piece of cheese and an unblown-up balloon. On the word 'Go!' they must drink the coffee, eat the cheese and blow up the balloon until it bursts. The first person to do this is considered the most sober, and he or she wins. It is, after all, a very good way to make the party end with a bang.

NUMBER OR YOUR LIFE △

Players: *any number*
Equipment: *none*

Players take turns to call out numbers, and the first player to call a suitable rejoinder gains a point. For example: 'One', – 'for the road'; 'Ten', – 'commandments'; 'Four', 'and twenty blackbirds'; Fifty-seven', – 'varieties'; and so on. The player who gains the most points wins. Numbers from one to twelve can be called as often as the players fancy, but numbers over twelve can only be put forward once in a game.

TEBAHPLA 〰

Players: *any number*
Equipment: *none*

This simple-sounding quickie is in fact more difficult than it appears. All the players have to do is to recite the alphabet in reverse, taking turns, with the first player starting at Z, the second saying Y, the third X, and so on round the group until A is reached and the players start again at Z. Any player who hesitates or says the wrong letter is eliminated. If the players survive three rounds, they must continue to repeat the alphabet backwards, but this time omitting all the letters whose capitals are written in print with one or more horizontal lines, i.e. Z, T, L, H, F, E, A. The last player left reciting the alphabet backwards wins.

TISSUE TOURNAMENT △

Players: *eight or more*
Equipment: *drinking straws for each player; pieces of tissue paper*

This hilarious game can either be played as a race, with two teams competing, or simply played for fun with the players standing in a circle. Each player holds a straw in his or her mouth. Assuming it is a team game, the leader of each team places a piece of tissue paper about six inches square over the end of the straw in his or her mouth and breathes in, thus causing the paper to be held in place at the end of the straw. The leader must then turn to the next player and pass the tissue paper on to him or her, the secret of a successful pass being that the first player must breathe out gently as the second player breathes in. Thus the paper must be passed along the whole line of the team, the first team to finish winning. The paper must not be touched by hand, but if it falls to the ground, as is likely, the player who dropped it is allowed to pick it up by hand and return it to its position at the end of his or her straw.

TONGUE-TWISTERS △

Players: *any number*
Equipment: *a stop-watch*

As guests make quarter-hearted efforts to help with the washing-up, while pulling on their hats and scarves, give the party a final fillip with a quick-fire round of tongue-twisters. If you want to be scrupulously fair, give each player the same twister, but if you want to make the game more interesting, give each a different one. Each player then has one minute in which to repeat his or her twister as many times as possible, and the player who crams the most correctly spoken twisters into his or her minute is the winner. The host or hostess must do the timing and the counting. Old favourites include 'Red lorry, yellow lorry', 'Cricket critic', 'If Peter Piper picked a peck of pickled pepper, where's the peck of pickled pepper Peter Piper picked', and so on. One of my favourites is, 'Can you imagine an imaginary menagerie manager imagining managing an imaginary menagerie?'